HOTELS and INNS OF LONG ISLAND'S NORTH FORK

Visitors arrive on Shelter Island at the dock of the famous Manhasset House Hotel. Ferries from nearby Greenport, Long Island, made this trip dozens of times a day during the tourist season. *Courtesy of the Southold Historical Society.*

HOTELS and INNS OF LONG ISLAND'S NORTH FORK

Geoffrey K. Fleming and Amy Kasuga Folk

The History Press

Published by The History Press
Charleston, SC 29403
www.historypress.net

First published 2009

Manufactured in the United States

ISBN 978.1.59629.725.8

Library of Congress Cataloging-in-Publication Data

Fleming, Geoffrey K.
Hotels and inns of Long Island's North Fork / Geoffrey K. Fleming and Amy Kasuga Folk.
p. cm.
Includes bibliographical references.
ISBN 978-1-59629-725-8
1. Hotels--New York (State)--North Fork (Peninsula)--History--Pictorial works. 2. Taverns (Inns)--New York (State)--North Fork (Peninsula)--History--Pictorial works. 3. Boardinghouses--New York (State)--North Fork (Peninsula)--History--Pictorial works. 4. Historic buildings--New York (State)--North Fork (Peninsula)--Pictorial works. 5. North Fork (N.Y. : Peninsula)--History, Local--Pictorial works. 6. Long Island (N.Y.)--History, Local--Pictorial works. I. Folk, Amy Kasuga. II. Title.
TX907.3.N72N674 2009
910.4609747'21--dc22
2009023594

Contents

The Prince Building, circa 1890s. The Prince Building was built by two enterprising individuals, Henry W. Prince (1839–1925) and G. Frank Hommel (1840–1909), each of whom occupied half of the first floor of the building. Prince's store had the first telephone exchange in Southold (1895) and was the home of the U.S. Post Office at least twice during its history. Today the structure holds the archives and serves as the headquarters of the Southold Historical Society. *Courtesy of the Southold Historical Society.*

Acknowledgements

This book is the first contemporary publication that documents the history of the many inns, taverns, hotels, boardinghouses, motels and bed-and-breakfasts that have served the tourist trade of the North Fork of Long Island for over 350 years.

Unlike other areas of local history, images of these hostelries are few and far between. That said, images used in this book were supplemented with original drawings, advertisements and other ephemera where appropriate and available.

This book is not meant to be a complete guide for all hotels that once stood on the North Fork; rather, it is merely meant to be a "slice" of 350+ years of history, a brief look at what was once a successful, if not booming, tourist phenomenon that took over and encompassed nearly every aspect of daily life beginning in the late nineteenth century.

A publication such as this one relies on the work of many different volunteers, as well as devoted and interested members of the public. While many of the images came from within the Southold Historical Society, a good deal of previously unrecorded photographs and information were provided by others. Thank you to Herbert Adler, Susan Barnes, Donald Boerum, Dottie Boyle, Mary "Penny" Coyle, Lois Cunliffe, Edward Dean, Anne Dixon, David and Daniel Folk, David Higbee, Walter Jackson, Joan Latham, Ellen Levin, Anne MacKay, Don McNeill, Ret and Allison Millis, Kerry Navarra, Gordon Rackett, Jim Rich, Richard Sledjeski, Edna Terry, Bob Patchell, Amy Uyanik, Ted Webb, Bob White, Elinor Williams, Susan

Cannon Young and all those here unnamed who helped provide information, images or inspiration for this book.

Special thanks are due to Melissa Andruski and Daniel McCarthy of the Southold Free Library's Whitaker Collection; Mariella Ostroski of the Cutchogue Free Library; Jeff Walden and Jerry Matovcik of the Mattituck-Laurel Library; Norman Wamback of the Mattituck–Laurel Historical Society; Ellen Cone-Busch of the Oysterponds Historical Society (the only local institution to preserve and maintain both an eighteenth-century tavern and a nineteenth-century boardinghouse); Edward H.L. Smith III and Wally Broege of the Suffolk County Historical Society; Bob Baumann of the Stirling Historical Society; Stacy Norklin and the Records Department at Southold Town Hall; Mike Verity and the Southold Town Building Department; and Wilfred Joseph of the North Fork Bed & Breakfast Association. We owe a debt of gratitude to all of the above who made information and images available for this project.

For those of you who have purchased this book: should you have or know someone who has photographic images of inns, taverns, hotels, boardinghouses or motels once located on the North Fork of Long Island, please consider sharing them with the society. We can be reached by mail at Southold Historical Society, PO Box 1, Southold, NY 11971 or on the web at www.southoldhistoricalsociety.org.

Geoffrey K. Fleming, Director
Southold Historical Society

Amy Kasuga Folk, Collections Manager
Southold Historical Society

INTRODUCTION

I suppose that in this day and age we are not that surprised when we see motels and hotels along the highways and byways of America. In many ways, we are spoiled by the ease with which we are able to find a place to spend the night. This was not always the case.

Though Long Island always had its share of taverns and inns located along the major mail and coach routes, there were few large hotels outside of the major metropolitan areas such as Brooklyn (yes, Brooklyn is on Long Island). The very first "tourist" hotels were built beginning in the late 1820s, but it was not until the period just after the Civil War that they became common (one of the first of this period was Tilyou's Surf House, erected in 1865, at Coney Island).

By the late nineteenth century, resorts constructed near the sandy beaches of Long Island had become centers for newly minted middle-class folks. They were places of respite away from the dirt, smog and crime of nearby urban centers. Many would at one time or another hold the title of "most elegant and fashionable hotel in the United States."

On Long Island's North Fork, we had everything going for us that much of the rest of the island had: beautiful beaches, ease of travel (since the Long Island Rail Road had come as far as Greenport) and picturesque villages and hamlets. But unlike many of our neighbors, we had a severe problem—the menhaden, or "bunker," industry.

Menhaden, also called bunkers, had been part of farming life on eastern Long Island since the late eighteenth century. They were used to fertilize farm fields between growing seasons, a process believed to have been first learned from the Native American populations that resided on the island. In the early days, the fish would be drawn to shore using huge fishing nets called haul seines. Farmers would then load their share into wagons and cart the fish to their farms, where they would be laid on the fields to help replenish the soil.

Eventually, the harvesting of menhaden became a bigger business, with companies, ships and teams organized to haul in the fish and transfer them to local factories constructed along the bay front. In the 1870s, steamers were employed not only to use purse seines to capture the fish, but also to carry them to the factories for processing. It was at these facilities that the resulting oil could be turned into a number of other products to be used in the manufacture of paint, preservatives and other goods. Local resident Joseph N. Hallock wrote in his memoir, *Southold Reminiscences*, concerning the existence of one of these factories on Great Hog Neck in Southold. In his memoir he stated, "In the days long ago, before I can remember, there was a fish factory on the east side of the very tip of Paradise Point, owned and operated by Jake Appley. It burned down, and I remember seeing the ruins."

The result of all this activity was an unbelievable stench that would hang around seemingly forever. This was especially a problem for the first boardinghouses that had sprung up on nearby Shelter Island, as bunker season coincided with the summer tourist season. This problem would hamper all efforts to establish a burgeoning hotel and resort industry on the North Fork.

The environment would finally change in the early 1880s, when many of the factories here were closed and moved to the northern coast of Long Island's South Fork. A location at Napeaque, near Montauk, had been selected years earlier since it was so distant from any large populations that would be affected by the odor created by processing menhaden. It also had a deep-water harbor perfect for the ships that would need to bring the fish there. By 1879, the first factories were built, with more added during the next two decades. The area where the factories were constructed was dubbed "The Promised Land," perhaps, as one historian noted, because it "smelled to high heaven and was the destination of bands of seasonal pilgrims; itinerant laborers looking for work."

With the menhaden industry moved elsewhere, the construction and establishment of new, more extravagant hotels could begin. This was welcome news as many of the older hotels, such as Mattituck House in

Mattituck hamlet, had been overcrowded for some time. Newspapers of the period noted that the hotel was so hopelessly overbooked for the summer season during this period that other local residents had to open up their houses to help board the many people who arrived in town and could not get hotel rooms.

By the early twentieth century, the costal bays of the North Fork were filled with new and enterprising hostelries. From the Miamogue and the Great Peconic Bay House in Jamesport, to the Clark House and Wyandank in Greenport, the area offered some of the finest accommodations outside of New York City. As the decades of the century progressed, hotels would give way to more boardinghouses, and they in turn to motels and eventually bed-and-breakfasts. During the Depression, many hotels would become speakeasies or brothels to help ensure their survival.

This book attempts to document just a small fraction of the many types of accommodations that were once available on Long Island's North Fork as well as providing notice of those that exist today. The owners of these hotels and inns continue the tradition of the human need for a clean, safe and pleasant place to rest after a weary day's travel. It takes a great deal of effort, and humility, to run a hotel. As internationally known culinary expert Graham Kerr (b. 1934) once noted: "My parents were in the hotel business, and I just loved the warm hearted people who worked so hard with such good humor."

Geoffrey K. Fleming, Director
Southold Historical Society

CHAPTER ONE

Early Inns and Taverns

From the first days of settlement, sustenance would have been an issue for the European settlers who came to the North Fork. Construction of shelters was imperative, though today we do not know exactly what kinds they built. They could have followed the customs of the local Indian populace, or may have immediately relied upon European tradition to build the first houses located here. The John Budd house, also known as the "Old House," is one of the oldest surviving houses on Long Island, having been built in Southold in 1649, just nine years after the initial settlement of the hamlet. It is, as one historian noted, "notable as one of the most distinguished surviving examples of English domestic architecture in America." With its small diamond-paned windows, low ceilings and clapboarded exterior, it is a model of what many structures in Southold looked like during the late seventeenth century.

Inns played an important role in the community early on, as those traveling to Boston found it easier to do so by taking hired boats or ferries from Orient Point, located at the very tip of Long Island's North Fork, than traveling up through Connecticut. It took several days to maneuver across the island, making rest stops for food, ale and sleep a necessity. The trip from landing spots in Queens to the village of Orient took an average of two to three full days, depending on weather and road conditions. This was the case as recently as the mid-nineteenth century and only ceased when the Long Island Rail Road (LIRR) was created and large, mechanically powered ferries became more common.

In Southold Town, as required by law, all tavern keepers had to pay for and acquire licenses on an annual basis. These licenses provided much-needed tax revenue for the town and ensured that there would never be too many taverns attracting unwanted visitors. Taverns provided a social gathering place for residents outside of church services as well as allowed travelers to rest and recoup after long journeys. Considering how strictly religious Southold was during the first century after settlement, it is novel to note that the primary drink of choice was rum, regardless of class or station. Part of this was due to the fact that rum could be, in some circumstances, safer to drink than the water.

By the mid-eighteenth century, there were dozens of taverns located across Southold Town, which stretched all the way from Wading River to Orient Point. Each hamlet or village had at least one primary tavern, which was nearly always supplemented by additional establishments located nearby.

Apparently, during the eighteenth century, there was a difference between tavern operators and the "retailers" who sold rum but did not operate taverns. Retailers could not sell rum in lesser amounts than a gallon—and most of the time it was sold by "the jugful." Some records indicate that rum could be acquired locally in such sizes as a "hogshead," a unit of measurement defined as a cask of sixty-three gallons, though these were often parceled out to various residents in a given community or area of the town. Taverns individually sold rum in much smaller portions, seemingly either by the "can" or "mug," to waiting customers.

One of the most celebrated establishments was the one known as Moore's Tavern, located on the corner of Boisseau Avenue and Route 25 in Southold village. It was associated with many notables, including Benjamin Franklin (1706–1790), John Ledyard (1751–1789) and a famous Hamilton. Dr. Alexander Hamilton (1715–1756), the noted diarist (not of federal fame), wrote about his stay at the tavern in 1744 during a trip from Maryland to Boston. Hamilton recorded the following about his stop in Southold:

> *We put up att one Mrs. More's in Southold. In her house appeared nothing but industry. She and her grandaughters were busied in carding and spinning of wool…Att night the house was crowded with a company of patched coats and tattered jackets, and consequently the conversation consisted chiefly of "Damne ye, Jack" and "Here's to you Tom"…* [after meeting a doctor and peddler]… *We left this company att 9 a'clock att night and went up stairs to bed, all in one chamber.*

Moore's Tavern, Southold, circa 1900. Known for much of its life as the "1640 House," the residential cape that operated as Moore's Tavern during the eighteenth century was actually completed about 1652 for Henry Case, one of the early settlers of Southold. Originally located on the south side of Route 25, the house was later moved a short distance to the north side near the corner of Boisseau Avenue. It was the site of the first skirmish of the American Revolution in Southold, when British soldiers were ambushed at the tavern by a group of men led by Captain Hart of Cutchogue. The British were eventually forced to retreat back to their boats, having lost eleven men. The tavern, which survived for over 280 years, was demolished in 1936. *Courtesy of the Southold Historical Society.*

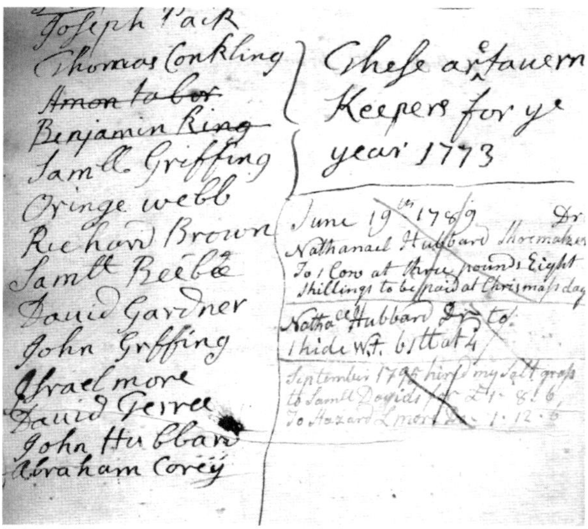

Joseph Pack
Thomas Conkling
~~Amon Tabor~~
Benjamin King
Saml Griffing
Oringe Webb
Richard Brown
Samll Beebe
David Gardner
John Griffing
Israel Moore
David Peirce
John Hubbard
Abraham Corey

These are tavern Keepers for ye year 1773

June 19th 1789 Dr
Nathanael Hubbard Shoemaker
To 1 Cow at three pounds Eight Shillings to be paid at Christmass day

List of tavern operators, Southold, 1773. As noted in the upper right corner of this image, "These are tavern Keepers for ye year 1773." The taverns in Southold were located around the many small hamlets and villages that made up the township. Each tavern had to be licensed to operate, and fees were due annually. During the late eighteenth century, members of the Landon family served as collectors of the tavern license fees for Southold. *Courtesy of the Oysterponds Historical Society.*

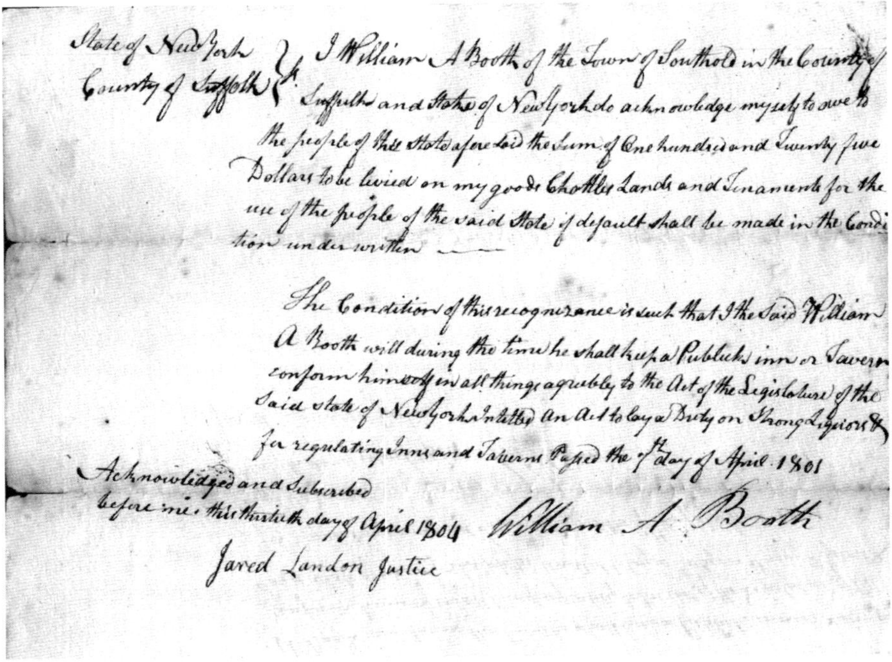

State of New York } ss. I William A Booth of the Town of Southold in the County of
County of Suffolk } Suffolk and State of New York do acknowledge myself to owe to
the people of the State aforesaid the sum of One hundred and Twenty five
Dollars to be levied on my goods Chattles Lands and Tenaments for the
use of the people of the said State if default shall be made in the Condi
tion under written —

The Condition of this recognizance is such that I the said William
A Booth will during the time he shall keep a Publick inn or Tavern
conform himself in all things agreeably to the Act of the Legislature of the
said state of New York intitled An Act to lay a Duty on Strong Liquors &
for regulating Inns and Taverns Passed the 7 day of April 1801

Acknowledged and Subscribed
before me this thirtieth day of April 1804 William A Booth
Jared Landon Justice

Tavern license, Southold, 1804. This image shows a typical tavern license for the early nineteenth century. William A. Booth pledged all his "goods, chattels, lands, and tenements" to the people of the State of New York should he default on the requirements set forth for those operating a "Publick inn or tavern." This requirement was part of a new law passed in 1801, which regulated the duties on "strong liquors" and the operation of "inns and taverns" by the state legislature. *Courtesy of the Oysterponds Historical Society.*

Opposite, top: Constant Booth Inn, Greenport, circa 1920. Constructed in 1720 in Sterling (also spelled Stirling, later to be rechristened Greenport), near Sterling Creek, this grand edifice served as the residence of William Booth (circa 1670–1722) and later his son, Lieutenant Constant Booth (1700–1774). It was here, in 1757, that a young George Washington, on his way to Boston via New London, stopped to rest. The inn was acquired in 1786 by Captain Orange Webb (1730–1805), who was a licensed tavern keeper in Southold as early as 1773. In the very late eighteenth century or early nineteenth century, the house was moved to a plot located at the intersection of the present Greenport Main Street and Route 25. *Courtesy of the Oysterponds Historical Society.*

Opposite, bottom: Constant Booth Inn, Orient, circa 1965. During the 1820s, this building left the ownership of the Webb family and a succession of new owners ensued. By the 1950s, the house, which was owned at the time by the Sinuta family, was in a derelict state. This was a period when many grand residences along the main roads of Southold were demolished and replaced by shopping centers and other new buildings. In 1955, the inn was saved by George Latham and was moved by barge to property he owned in the village of Orient (now Poquatuck Park). Since 1981, the former tavern has been open to the public and operated by the Oysterponds Historical Society. *Courtesy of the Oysterponds Historical Society.*

CHAPTER TWO

ORIENT POINT INN

At the far eastern end of the North Fork is the community of Orient. Originally known as Oysterponds, the area changed its name to Orient in 1837 because of the frequent misdirection of the mail to Oyster Bay. Natives of the area have always divided themselves between those who live in the Village and those who live at the Point. The community, which is spread over four miles of peninsula, during severe storms was frequently cut off from the rest of the North Fork. Situated almost at the tip of the Point is the former site of the famous Orient Point Inn.

The inn was originally built about 1672 as a small home, and during the American Revolution the house was used to quarter British troops. The English also built a small fort to overlook Plum Gut on the high land behind the house. The noted historian Augustus Griffin wrote in his famous journal how British soldiers, in a show of power, transported several cannons through the village on their way to the Point to fortify the new emplacement. It wasn't until 1834 that the small house was formally turned into a stop for travelers by Jonathan Fish Latham. The house was named the Orient Point House and was enlarged to accommodate guests looking to stay overnight on their journey by boat to and from Connecticut. Latham ran the inn until his death in 1853, when it was sold at auction by his ten children.

The business went through a series of owners until Anna Brownson, who purchased the building in 1860, gave the business to her niece Elizabeth Parsons in 1862. The inn began to attract more than just customers passing through the area. It developed a reputation of fine dining and comfortable rooms and was becoming popular with hunters, fishermen and visitors looking for solitude. While staying at the hotel in 1860, James Fenimore Cooper wrote his novel *Sea Lions*, and in it he described the area as the most secluded spot on the whole island. The poet Walt Whitman and the famous orator Daniel Webster were also reported to have visited the inn.

In 1878, the inn was sold to Merry Parsons, who advertised the hotel through the Montauk Steamboat Company and Curtain's business directory. In the post–Civil War world, people looking to escape the unhealthy air of New York City and its environs began coming to the East End and the Orient Point Inn in droves. Local letters and diaries from this period mention that the inn, when full, would send guests with clean linens to stay at the homes of local residents.

From 1887 to 1921, the hotel again went through a series of owners until 1922, when Eugene McDonnell, who also ran another large hotel in Orient, Mount Pleasant House, purchased the inn. During this time period, a number of famous people were said to have visited the inn, including President Grover Cleveland, actress Sarah Bernhardt and former First Lady Edith Roosevelt.

In September 1938, one of the largest hurricanes to hit the East End struck and devastated the area. The Orient Point Inn, like many other buildings in the area, lost its roof and flooded as the ocean rose and covered the Point. McDonnell repaired the damage to the building and rebuilt the roofline of the main section of the building, eliminating the cupola.

McDonnell ran the inn until the 1950s, when New York State mandated that all hotels taller than one story needed to have a steel reinforced frame. The inn, which had grown to three stories and had retained its timber framed structure, closed it doors.

By the 1970s, the abandoned structure was rotting and starting to collapse on itself. A developer had purchased the property and sought permission to wreck what was left of the building and put up a series of condos. The residents of Orient fought to save the historic building, which in the end was deemed on the verge of collapse and was taken down for safety reasons. Today, the site is a park.

Orient Point House, circa 1870. The Orient Point Inn during its heyday. The inn's image appeared on the top of an advertising poster beckoning city people to travel down Long Island Sound on the Montauk Steamboat Company's steamer *W.W. Coit* to the Point. *Courtesy of the Oysterponds Historical Society.*

Admission ticket to a ball at the Orient Point House, circa 1865–70. The inn was a popular meeting and entertainment center for guests and local groups alike. This ticket was presented to Albert Corwin (b. 1837), a Civil War veteran from Peconic. *Courtesy of the Southold Historical Society.*

Orient Point Inn, circa 1880. The approach to the hotel from the west, looking east. This is the way overland travelers coming from the Greenport railroad station or tourists staying in nearby Orient Village would have first seen the inn. *Courtesy of the Oysterponds Historical Society.*

Orient Point Inn, circa 1900. A view of the front with a swing set, this image was probably taken during the height of the season. Note the awnings over each window, which helped repel the strong afternoon sunlight. *Courtesy of the Oysterponds Historical Society.*

Orient Point Inn, circa 1900. As it looked at the turn of the century, when the inn was still attracting a large number of tourists from the cities and quite a few residents from the surrounding villages, who would come to "visit" for the weekend. *Courtesy of the Oysterponds Historical Society.*

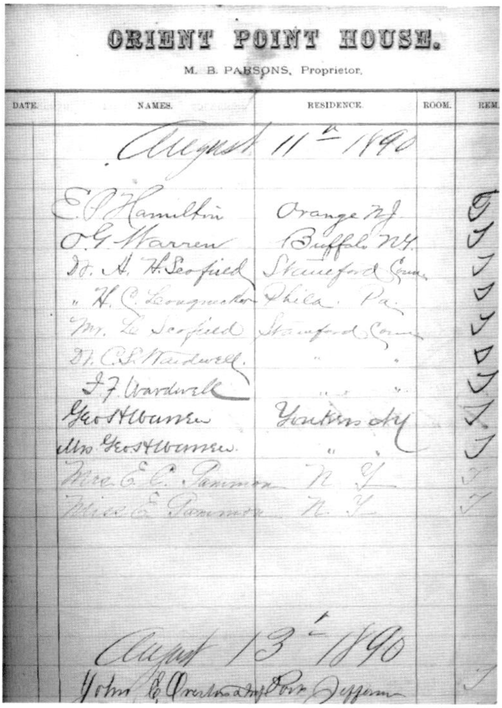

ORIENT POINT HOUSE.

M. B. PARSONS, Proprietor.

DATE.	NAMES.	RESIDENCE.	ROOM.	REM.
	August 11th 1890			
	E. P. Hamilton	Orange N.J.		
	O. G. Warren	Buffalo N.Y.		
	D. A. H. Scofield	Stamford Conn		
	" H. C. Longmaker	Phila. Pa.		
	Mr. L. Scofield	Stamford Conn		
	D. C. S. Wardwell	"		
	J. F. Wardwell	"		
	Geo H Banner	Yonkers N.Y.		
	Mrs Geo H Banner	"		
	Mrs E. C. Pammon	N. Y.		
	Miss E. Pammon	N. Y.		
	August 13th 1890			
	John E. [illegible]	Port Jefferson		

A page from the register of the Orient Point Inn, 1890. This page shows guests from not only the Long Island area but also distant parts of New York, New Jersey, Connecticut and Pennsylvania. *Courtesy of the Oysterponds Historical Society.*

Orient Point Inn, 1938. Shown after the great 1938 hurricane, which destroyed so many homes and devastated many New England communities. Furniture scavenged from the aftermath of the storm has been set out to dry. Note in the background that the roof of the center section of the building is missing, having been lifted off and deposited elsewhere. *Courtesy of the Oysterponds Historical Society.*

Orient Point Inn, circa 1940. After the renovations and repairs from the 1938 hurricane. Note the changes in the roofline of the center section of the building—now peaked instead of flat. The once prominent cupola was never replaced. Other minor changes in the windows can be seen on the ends of the building. *Courtesy of the Oysterponds Historical Society.*

Orient Point Inn, 1959. A watercolor of the building by Joseph Di Gemma, who had established a studio in Southold in 1949. The building was a popular subject in painting as well as photography. *Courtesy of the Oysterponds Historical Society.*

Orient Point Inn, circa 1960. A view of the building not long before it closed. The structure was still imposing, but was in the modern age a white elephant, too big to be a residence and too expensive to renovate to comply with commercial use. *Courtesy of the Oysterponds Historical Society.*

Orient Point Inn, circa 1950. "The Dignity of Age"—a posed postcard advertising the inn. The card shows the fireplace in the front lobby of the hotel and the appeal of the peace and quiet serenity of the Point. *Courtesy of the Oysterponds Historical Society.*

Orient Point Inn, circa 1970. This image shows the same room as the postcard "The Dignity of Age." After years of neglect, the walls and the fireplace have collapsed. *Courtesy of the Oysterponds Historical Society.*

Orient Point Inn, circa 1970. The front porch has collapsed and is blocking the front door. It was shortly after this picture was taken that the structure was bulldozed, having been deemed a public hazard. *Courtesy of the Oysterponds Historical Society.*

CHAPTER THREE

HOTELS

As time marched on over the course of the nineteenth century, Long Island gradually became less of a path to other places and more of an end destination. At the opening of the century, Long Island was made up of loosely connected rural communities. Most communities existed along the north and south shores of the island, connected to one another by water routes and the three main roads that were originally laid out in 1733 (North Country Road, Middle Country Road and South Country Road). The center of the island was sparsely settled.

By 1844, the Long Island Rail Road, conceived of as a way of speeding travelers to and from New York City to Boston, spurred the development of the inn-keeping business on the North Fork. While most villages prior to the Civil War had perhaps one inn for the wandering traveler, Greenport, the terminus of the railroad, had seven hotels and several boardinghouses. Standing side by side and across the street from one another, next to the railroad station in Greenport stood the Peconic Bay House, Wyandank House and Sterlington Hotel, all on what is now Third Street by the Shelter Island ferry dock. On the other side of town, establishments such as the Timson Hotel, Booth House, Mott's Commercial Hotel and Clarke House competed for guests disembarking from the steamships that regularly traveled between New York City and the East End. By 1910, these businesses had been joined by four more hotels.

Shortly after the Civil War, vacations and travel stopped being a privilege of just the wealthy as an increasing number of workers began to have more leisure time. Mechanization was becoming more common in a larger number of occupations, thus decreasing the labor-intensive work of many jobs. It became fashionable for city dwellers to travel to the seaside to get away from the foul air and waves of disease that periodically swept through the densely populated neighborhoods of New York City. In response to the increasing number of visitors, larger and larger hotels began to spring up all over Long Island to accommodate these new tourists.

Hotels on the East End were in competition with tourist resorts not only across the south shore of Long Island but also with a number of hotels in the Catskill Mountains and hotels that sprang up around "medicinal" hot springs, such as Saratoga Springs in upstate New York, as well as vacation areas on the New Jersey seashore. By the turn of the century, newspapers in New York City regularly printed a large variety of advertisements from hotels scattered around the countryside surrounding the city. In addition to advertising in the papers, North Fork hotels also had advertising cards and posters made to attract business.

Holding back the newly fledged tourist trade was the overpowering fish smell that permeated the North Fork from spring to fall from the menhaden "bunker" fishing trade. When the bunker processing industry departed, the hotel business on the North Fork grew as tourists began to come in larger and larger numbers. Responding to the influx, new hotel buildings began to spring up double and triple in size compared to previous inns on the North Fork. Inns such as the Great Peconic Bay House, the Mononotto and Orient Point built or expanded their establishments to maximize their capacity. Often successful hotels were leased to others to manage when the original owners tired of the business.

On the North Fork, one of the legal definitions of a hotel is that it could sell liquor on its premises. In fact, many hotels had one or more bars. The larger hotels boasted of having many of the amenities we today think of in only the most expensive resorts, including bars, beauty shops, barbershops, tailors, game rooms, restaurants, ballrooms and live music entertainment.

Guests who came to the North Fork could enjoy not only the beautiful water views and sandy bay beaches, but also the rocky sound shores and rural vistas. Most villages also had a number of bars and restaurants that catered to tourists. In 1907, the Oak Grove Casino opened in Greenport at the end of Ninth Street, which featured dance contests and bathhouses on the beach. For people who enjoyed watching horses, there was also harness racing available. Visitors had a choice among Israel Peck's Spruce Park/Oaklawn track in Southold, the Greenport track between Sixth Street and Cherry Lane (Ninth Street) and Peconic's Indian Neck Driving Club track, which by 1909 was featuring races every Saturday.

Great Peconic Bay House, South Jamesport, circa 1906. Built in 1878 by Captain Edward Downs, the hotel was a massive four stories tall with one hundred rooms. Situated at the foot of South Jamesport Avenue, the building had water views on three sides. In 1902, the hotel was advertised as "the best equipped" with the "finest location in this section [of Long Island]." *Courtesy of Norman Wamback.*

Hanging sign from Great Peconic Bay House, circa 1890s. *Private collection, Southold.*

Site of the Great Peconic Bay House, South Jamesport, circa 2008. The business closed in 1952, and after being vacant for many years, the hotel was taken down in the late 1950s. The remains of the wharf, which had been built in 1833 and stood in front of the hotel, can still be seen on the wide swath of sandy beach. *Courtesy of Norman Wamback.*

Shore front, South Jamesport, circa 1906. The dock and yacht club building (shown at far left) in front of the Miamogue Hotel. Like at many other large hotels, guests had many recreational options, including sailing on Peconic Bay. *Courtesy of Norman Wamback.*

Shoreline of South Jamesport, circa 1912. This view of the dock and harbor of South Jamesport shows the Great Peconic Bay House and the Miamogue Hotel in the distance. Note the many small buildings that once dotted the shore. *Courtesy of Norman Wamback.*

Miamogue Hotel, South Jamesport, circa 1907. The first incarnation of this hotel was built in 1875 and it was the first large hotel in South Jamesport. Owned by I. Seymour Corwin, the building was destroyed by fire in 1895. The fire began in a neighbor's kitchen at 1:30 a.m., and firemen worked to contain the fire with water from the Miamogue Hotel's waterworks, which stood on the opposite corner of the street, when a spark set the roof of the hotel on fire. When the fire was finally contained, only the livery stable remained from the hotel complex. The main hotel building and its annex were both destroyed. *Courtesy of Norman Wamback.*

The Miamogue Hotel, South Jamesport, L. I.

Miamogue Hotel and the Great Peconic Bay House, South Jamesport, circa 1905. Note how close together the two hotels were located in the small village of Jamesport. Besides the two hotels seen here, South Jamesport also had three other smaller hotels. Altogether at the height of the season, up to six hundred tourists could comfortably stay in the village. *Courtesy of the Southold Historical Society.*

Opposite, top: Miamogue Hotel, South Jamesport, front view, circa 1900. After being consumed in the fire, the hotel was rebuilt in 1897, and the new complex included an illuminating gas plant. The owner expanded the hotel complex by buying a smaller competitor, the Sunnyside House, and knocking it down. The new Miamogue rivaled the Great Peconic Bay House in size. The owner, I. Seymour Corwin, passed away in South Jamesport in February 1926 at the age of seventy-five when he fell and hit his head on the ice. The second building was again destroyed by fire in 1932 and was not rebuilt. *Courtesy of Norman Wamback.*

Opposite, bottom: Shoreline of South Jamesport, circa 2008. A modern view of the site of the Miamogue Hotel. *Courtesy of Norman Wamback.*

Glenwood Hotel, Mattituck, circa 1907. This hotel was built in 1860, and the building started out as the summer house of the Samuel Sneden family of Brooklyn. In 1892, the house was sold and converted into a hotel by John Zenzius. By 1895, Zenzius had sold the business to Clement MacMillan. *Courtesy of Norman Wamback.*

Glenwood Lodge, Mattituck, circa 1919. Formerly the Glenwood Hotel, the building was renamed in 1919 when the hotel was sold again. It operated as a hotel until 1962. In 2004, the building, which had stood vacant for a number of years, was renovated and turned into offices in downtown Mattituck. *Courtesy of Cutchogue New Suffolk Library.*

Mattituck House, Mattituck, circa 1905. This successful hotel was owned by a series of owners, including the Riley brothers, William Niederstein, George Blake, Edith Peyton and Carl Dahl. It stood across the street from the Mattituck Presbyterian Church on Love Lane. The original section of the building was constructed in the 1700s, and was more than doubled in size during the nineteenth century. George Washington visited the inn in 1751 on his way to Stirling (Greenport), and Thomas Jefferson and James Madison also visited the hotel. The building had thirty-two rooms, and by the turn of the century it offered automobile service to the beach and its three bathhouses. The owners even boasted about its duck and lobster dinners. The hotel was eventually taken down and its site is currently occupied by a small store and public parking. *Courtesy of Norman Wamback.*

Eureka Hotel, Mattituck, circa 1900. Built in the 1860s for George Brown, the building changed hands several times until 1885, when it was purchased by Clement MacMillan and turned into the Eureka House hotel. The building still stands just north of the railroad tracks in Mattituck. *Courtesy of Norman Wamback.*

New Suffolk Hotel, New Suffolk, circa 1950. Also known as MacNish's or Grant's Hotel, the inn was started by William MacNish, and was eventually sold to William H. Grant in 1893. Grant worked in Brooklyn and traveled to New Suffolk (located between Peconic and Cutchogue) every summer with his family to run the hotel. At the turn of the century, the hotel closed and the building was divided up and sold to various owners, with the main section of the building moved to a lot two blocks east, where it was abandoned and eventually collapsed. This hotel stood in New Suffolk, where the baseball diamond is located today. *Courtesy of the Southold Historical Society.*

Southold Hotel, Southold, circa 1880. This building was originally constructed about 1830 as a store for William Homan Wells (b. 1806) near the corner of Main Road and Youngs Avenue. He was the first to incorporate a hotel with the store, and it was operated during its first years under a partnership with William Albertson and William Fythian. Wells bought out the partners in the mid-1850s and operated the hotel with his son, J. Albert Wells (1836–1897), until 1868. In 1873, the property was sold to J. Wickham, who in turn sold

it to Frank Judd in 1875. Judd enlarged the hotel further, in addition to adding a croquet lawn and new trees and plantings. In 1870, the *Long Island Traveler* newspaper noted that the Southold Hotel was so popular that the proprietor was forced to find accommodations for many of his additional guests in the private homes of the village. *Courtesy of the Southold Historical Society.*

Portrait of William Homan Wells, circa 1840. Wells (1806–1871) was the owner of the Southold Hotel, which stood on the site of the original home lot of the first William Wells, one of the early settlers of Southold. William H. Wells was a successful businessman, auctioneer and a keeper of the Wells genealogy. The portrait, though unsigned, may have been painted by noted Sag Harbor portraitist Hubbard Latham Fordham. *Courtesy of the Southold Historical Society.*

Above: Coins for the bar at the Southold Hotel, given out to guests for a free drink at the hotel bar. *Courtesy of the Southold Historical Society.*

Below: A wallet advertising the fifteenth anniversary (1898–1913) of the Southold Hotel under Theodore Hoinkis's management. *Courtesy of the Southold Historical Society.*

Southold Hotel, Southold, circa 1900. The final owner of the hotel was Theodore Hoinkis, who arrived from New Jersey to operate the business until it closed. During his tenure, the building could accommodate up to twenty-five guests. Following the closure of the hotel, the building was dismantled in 1926, and various sections were moved to other parts of Southold. Not long after, the Southold Savings Bank was built on the site. *Courtesy of the Southold Historical Society.*

SOUTHOLD HOTEL

Albertson Livery Stable, Southold, circa 1900. Stables like this one were essential for many of the hotels and boardinghouses in Southold, as they provided much-needed room for the horses that guests required before the days of automobiles. The stable was owned by Corey Albertson and stood around the corner from the Southold Hotel, on the east side of Youngs Avenue across from Traveler Street. Standing in front of the stable are (left to right) Corey Albertson, Harry Howell and Clinton Carrole. The building was replaced by a large brick and glass building in the 1980s, which was built to house the Mortgage Division of Southold Savings Bank. *Courtesy of the Southold Historical Society.*

Opposite, top: Cedar Beach Inn–General Wayne Inn, Southold, circa 1958. This house was built in 1784 for a Major Horton. The building and surrounding property was purchased in the early twentieth century by Edwin H. Brown for the newly formed Reydon Country Club, and the structure was to be renovated as a clubhouse. Before the building was used by the club, Brown decided to move to another, nearby location. The building was then converted into the Cedar Beach Inn. In 1949, Eugene Sutherland of East Marion purchased the property from Howard Toedter of New York City. The property—which had consisted of 175 acres, including the inn and seven other buildings, as well as farmland and waterfront property—was then subdivided and sold off. *Courtesy of the Southold Historical Society.*

Opposite, bottom: Interior of the Cedar Beach Inn, Southold, 1958. This image shows the dining room in the General Wayne set for guests. *Courtesy of the Southold Historical Society.*

Advertisement for the Cedar Beach Inn, Southold, circa 1930. The inn is located on one of the small inlets off of Peconic Bay in the Bayview section of Southold. It advertised a wide range of water sports as well as golf, tennis and riding. In 1998, the inn was renamed the General Wayne Hotel by new owners, in honor of General Anthony Wayne of the American Revolution. Today, the hotel is abandoned and partially demolished. *Courtesy of the Southold Historical Society.*

Opposite, top: Conway's Horton Point House, Southold, 2009. All that remains of this once grand hotel is this small section, now converted to a private residence. Opened in 1869, the hotel offered forty rooms and was operated by the Conway family. The original building was located west of Horton Point Lighthouse on the bluffs that overlook Long Island Sound. Mrs. J. Conway advertised the farm fresh produce that was available at the hotel, as well as the good shooting that could be had nearby. In 1906, the hotel was acquired by Walter Clark and later by the Hyatt family. *Courtesy of the Southold Historical Society.*

Kreutzer's Park Hotel, Southold, circa 1919. The Kreutzer family, a Brooklyn family of German descent, arrived in Southold sometime after the Civil War and operated a farm. In the late 1890s or early 1900s, they established their new hotel on land known as the "Old Field." Located on the south side of Route 25 in Southold, the elaborate Italianate-style building included three full stories as well as an annex where the dining/entertainment hall was located, along with additional rooms. To the left rear of the hotel was the large and ornate outhouse, which was able to accommodate many people in a single sitting. *Courtesy of Old Field Vineyard.*

Kreutzer's Park Hotel, Southold, circa 1910. This postcard shows both the main building and the annex, which was located next door. During this period, the hotel, which also offered a saloon, was operated by the widow Marie Kreutzer (b. 1855). The hotel had a dance team of two women, named Mabel & Curly, who were apparently a little too risqué for Southold—many local wives hoped that someone would purchase the hotel and close it so that their husbands would stay away from the flirtatious showgirls. *Courtesy of Old Field Vineyard.*

Kreutzer's Park Hotel, Southold, circa 1920–21. The women of Southold would not have to wait long for their prayers to be answered. After much negotiation, the Lang family acquired the Kreutzer hotel in 1919. Like the Kreutzers, they were also from Brooklyn and had made their money in the dry goods business. They began plans to convert the building into a summer estate. The top floor of the hotel was removed and the two lower floors were rolled down to the water, south of where the original hotel had stood. *Courtesy of Old Field Vineyard.*

The Lang residence, Southold, circa 1921. The vision behind the conversion of the Kreutzer hotel into a residence was that of Mathilde Stricker Lang. A frugal woman, she reused as much of the lumber as possible in reworking the old hotel into her new summer estate. This included taking the old window frames, removing the glass, moving one muntin, adding two more and reinserting them into the building. These alterations, along with other changes, helped her achieve a more colonial look for her new home. Today, the home continues to be owned by the Lang descendants and is the centerpiece of their business enterprise, the Old Field Vineyard. *Courtesy of Old Field Vineyard.*

Kreutzer's dining hall, Southold, circa 1924. At the same time, the original annex building was altered in a different manner. Here, the first story was removed and the top two floors were lowered to the ground. The building is shown as work continued on settling it into its new position. *Courtesy of Old Field Vineyard.*

Peter Gaffga, circa 1924. Gaffga was a local resident who worked on the conversion of the former Kreutzer's Park Hotel buildings. He is shown here standing in front of the recently lowered annex structure. The building would serve as part of the farm complex, which until recent years was extensive, including acreage on both sides of Route 25. *Courtesy of Old Field Vineyard.*

Sunrise Hotel, Southold, 1945. This Second Empire–style building was built prior to 1909 and may have been originally the home of J.M. Post. The house became the Sunrise Hotel, then the French restaurant La Gazelle and then Coeur de Vignes. Currently it is the hotel and restaurant North Fork Table and Inn. *Courtesy of the Southold Historical Society.*

Interior of the Sunrise Hotel, Southold, 1945. The dining room of the Sunrise Hotel, showing one of the original archways and fireplaces. *Courtesy of the Southold Historical Society.*

Clarke House, Greenport, circa 1881. The hotel was built in 1831 and stood on Main Street. Started by John Clarke, the house was originally an early tavern in the village of Stirling. Shortly after it opened, it was the site of a meeting of village residents who voted to change the name of the village from Stirling to "Green Port." *Courtesy of the Southold Free Library.*

Clarke House, Greenport, circa 1906. The fountain seen in the foreground of the image is still standing, west of where the hotel once stood. The fountain was given to Greenport in 1905 as a memorial for Isaac Reeves, and in 1967 it collapsed from the ravages of time and was moved in from the edge of the street and restored by the village. *Courtesy of the Oysterponds Historical Society.*

THE CLARK HOUSE,
GREENPORT, L. I., SEPTEMBER 8, 1886.

ANNUAL REUNION OF CO. H, 127TH REGT., N. Y. S. V.

ATTENTION COMPANY!

"Give thanks always for all things unto God.—Eph. V, 20.

BOILED MUTTON, CAPER SAUCE

"DEPLOY AS SKIRMISHERS AGAINST THE FORAGE TRAINS."

BAKED BRIDGEPORT HAM — BAKED PIG

PRIME RIBS OF ROAST BEEF — ROAST TURKEY

BROILED CHICKEN — PORK AND BEANS — APPLE SAUCE

"RALLY ON THE RESERVE, TO ATTACK LINE OF SUPPLY."

BOILED POTATOES — MASHED POTATOES — SWEET POTATOES

STEWED CORN — LIMA BEANS

GLOVER SQUASH — BEETS — ONIONS

"Better is a dinner of herbs where love is, than a stalled ox and hatred therewith."
Prov XV, 17.

PICKLED ONIONS — CUCUMBERS — OLIVES — MIXED PICKLES

"ASSEMBLE ON COLOR COMPANY." "ARMS APORT!"

APPLE PIE — PUMPKIN PIE

"What calls back the past like the rich Pumpkin Pie?"—Whittier.

ALICE'S TAPIOCA PUDDING

ALICE'S FRENCH ROLLS — FRUIT CAKE — CITRON CAKE

MRS. BAKER'S PEACH ICE CREAM

SPONGE CAKE — FANCY CRACKERS

"All he wants now is sugar plums and rest."—Pope.

LAYER RAISINS — KISSES — NUTS

TEA — CHEESE — COFFEE

"Now good digestion wait on appetite, and health on all."—Shakespeare.

"RIGHT ABOUT FACE! PARADE DISMISSED!"

Menu from the Clarke House, Greenport, 1886. One of the largest Civil War units to be gathered on Long Island and sent south was the 127th New York State Volunteers. For years afterward, members of the Grand Army of the Republic (GAR), the veterans' association for Civil War soldiers, met annually for dinner in many inns and restaurants across the North Fork. The "kisses" noted at the bottom of the menu are a baked dessert of egg whites and powdered sugar. The popular chocolates known as kisses today didn't start being manufactured until 1907. *Courtesy of the Southold Free Library.*

Clarke House, Greenport, auction of contents, 1929. In 1845, with the building boom of hotels in the area, John Clarke added on to the hotel. The business was taken over by Clarke's daughters, Betsey and Susan, who ran it until 1927. In 1929, contents of the house were auctioned off and the structure was taken over by the Village. In 1935, the Village

of Greenport demolished the main section of the building and kept the kitchen wing as a police office until 1954, when it too was demolished to make way for a parking lot. *Courtesy of the Southold Free Library.*

Wyandank Hotel, Greenport, circa 1905. The Wyandank originally stood on Railroad Avenue (now Third Street) and was built in 1840. The building was four stories tall and had thirty rooms and a spacious dining room. The hotel had a series of owners, including S.P. Conklin, Charles C. Wright, Ansel V. Young and F.J. Corwin. Corwin, who later went on to own the Long Island House of Riverhead, owned the Wyandank from 1888 to 1893. The venerable Wyandank Hotel was demolished in 1968. *Courtesy of the Cutchogue New Suffolk Library.*

Wyandank Hotel, Greenport, with exterior water view inset, circa 1908. "Bring $20 and a clean shirt on the train and leave the same way" was a common saying passed around by some local residents about tourists who stayed in the hotels close to the railroad station. *Courtesy of the Cutchogue New Suffolk Library.*

Peconic Bay House, Greenport, circa 1860. Located across the street from the Wyandank and the Sterlington Hotels, the Peconic Bay House was situated on the edge of a waterfront park in Greenport. The Peconic Bay House was built in 1845 by John Webb, who was originally from Cutchogue. In 1860, F.B. Goldsmith owned the business and shared an advertisement with the owner of the Wyandank, not only promoting the charms of the area but also noting that a telegraph office was attached to the hotel for customers' convenience. *Courtesy of the Southold Free Library.*

Peconic Bay House, Greenport, circa 1900. In 1865, the Peconic Bay House was owned by L.O. Richardson and later by Augustus Smith. The hotel was demolished sometime prior to 1930. When local residents Will Robinson and John Verity took down the building, they salvaged enough wood from it to build five houses in Greenport. *Courtesy of the Southold Free Library.*

Booth House, Greenport, circa 1906. The hotel was used by the U.S. Coast Guard during World War II. In 1968, the building was sold and renovated to become a home for senior citizens. The renovations were never completed, and in early 1971, building plans changed to turn the building back into a restaurant and hotel. During the summer of that year, the building was put back on the market, and it burned down just as it was about to be sold again. Today, a condo unit is slated to be erected on the site of the former hotel. *Courtesy of the Oysterponds Historical Society.*

Booth House, Greenport, circa 1930. Built in 1877, the Booth House should not be confused with the Booth Inn (Webb House), which was moved to Orient. The building was three stories tall and had forty rooms. The hotel was situated just west of Ludlum Street in Greenport on the water. *Courtesy of the Oysterponds Historical Society.*

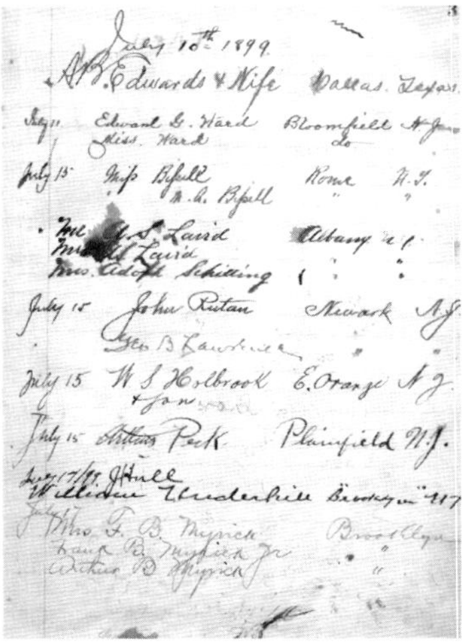
July 10th 1899
A. B. Edwards & Wife Dallas Texas
Newark N.J.
E. Orange N.J.
Plainfield N.J.

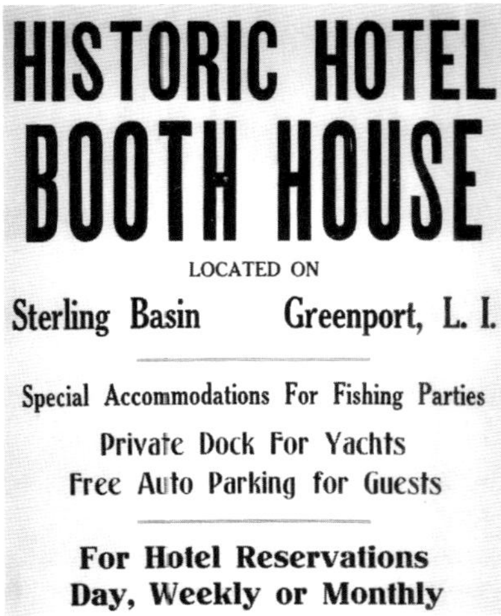

Above, left: Page from the Booth House register, 1899, showing guests from as far away as Dallas, Texas, as well as those from nearby New Jersey. *Courtesy of the Oysterponds Historical Society.*

Above, right: Advertising poster for the Booth House, circa 1935. This poster, which features a phone number, comes from the later period in the history of the hotel's life. *Courtesy of the Southold Historical Society.*

Griffing House, Greenport, circa 1900. The following trio of pictures shows the same building in three incarnations. The hotel stood on Front Street in Greenport next to the Vienna Hotel and Restaurant. The Griffing family, which included the local historian and innkeeper Augustus Griffin of Orient, has had a long tradition of hotel keeping on the North Fork, starting in the late 1700s. This establishment was undoubtedly run by the descendant of one of Augustus's many cousins. *Courtesy of the Oysterponds Historical Society.*

Hotel Dennis, Greenport, 1914. Run by Louis Victory from 1910 until just before 1920. Victory was unmarried and had a staff of three maids and one hired man to run the business. All of the staff were foreign born and ranged in age from seventeen to twenty-one. *Courtesy of the Cutchogue New Suffolk Library.*

Greenport House, Greenport, 1920. Interestingly, the previous image of the building as the Hotel Dennis and this image of it as the Greenport House are identical except for the sign. The photographer probably reused the earlier photograph to reproduce the card. *Courtesy of the Cutchogue New Suffolk Library.*

Dining room of the Vienna Hotel, Greenport, 1910. During the 1920s, the restaurant was extremely popular, and Douglas Fairbanks and Mary Pickford are said to have come out from Manhattan to eat there. In 1947, the business was sold to Edward McComber, who renamed it Hotel Greenport. *Courtesy of the Southold Historical Society.*

Vienna Hotel, Greenport, circa 1910. Run by Stephan Cvija, in 1910, this hotel and restaurant stood mid-block on Front Street in Greenport next to the Hotel Dennis. A modest three stories in height, the building featured a large restaurant on the ground floor with rooms above it. *Courtesy of the Southold Historical Society.*

RKET
DAY NIGHT til 9PM
HELEN'S
HOTEL
RESTAURANT
TELEVISION
WORTHS

STERLINGTON HOUSE, GREENPORT, L. I.

Mott's Hotel, Greenport, circa 1905–10. The building was originally known as the Greenport Hotel and was owned by Abraham Sully, who ran the business from 1880 to the 1900s and catered to sailors. The building was purchased by Mary M. Mott, a widow who owned and ran the hotel as the Commercial Hotel in 1910. *Courtesy of the Southold Historical Society.*

Opposite, top: Helen's Hotel, Greenport, 1941. This is a later incarnation of the Vienna Hotel. In addition to being Helen's Hotel, this was also known as Bill Worth's Restaurant, and in 1974 it became the Rhumbline Restaurant. *Courtesy of the Southold Historical Society.*

Opposite, bottom: Sterlington Hotel, Greenport, circa 1900. Originally named the Burr Hotel, the building was renamed the Sterlington in 1894. In 1910, it was owned by F.B. Thorn, and it stood next to the Wyandank on Third Street (then known as Railroad Avenue). The building still stands and currently houses a Mexican restaurant on the ground floor. *Courtesy of the Cutchogue New Suffolk Library.*

F.J. Claudio's, Greenport, circa 1915. The Claudio family arrived in the Greenport area in the late 1870s. Manuel Claudio was a liquor dealer on Main Street from 1880 to 1896, when he applied for a hotel license to expand his business, founding the Star Hotel.

Eventually Claudio and his son Frank purchased the Commercial Hotel and ran the business first as a hotel and restaurant combined and later as just a restaurant. *Courtesy of the Southold Historical Society.*

Above: Townsend Manor Inn, Greenport, circa 1970. The building was constructed between 1802 and 1850 for George Cogswell, a whaling captain. By 1850, Catherine Cogswell was living in the house alone. Lillian Cook Townsend purchased the property between 1916 and 1925 and converted the building into the Townsend Manor Inn, which it remains today. *Courtesy of the Oysterponds Historical Society.*

Left: Advertisement for Townsend Manor Inn, circa 1966. This ad was featured in a booklet aimed at tourists coming to the North Fork during the 1960s. *Courtesy of the Southold Historical Society.*

Timson Hotel, Greenport, circa 1882. The business started as the Jane Timson Hotel and was situated across the street from the junction of Main Street and Central Avenue. The hotel, which operated from 1869 to 1891, was started by James Timson, who may have named it after his second wife. The building was then sold to George N. Flack, who operated his painting and decorating business from the structure. For much of the twentieth century, the building housed the popular framing store managed by Everett J. Warner. *Private collection.*

Mount Pleasant House, Orient, circa 1880.
Built by William and Samuel Young in 1879, this building was originally designed to be a boardinghouse. The Young brothers sold the business to John and Joseph Miller in 1882. *Courtesy of the Oysterponds Historical Society.*

Mount Pleasant House, Orient, circa 1900. John Miller bought out his brother's side of the business and then expanded the building in 1883. About 1920, Eugene McDonnell, later the owner of the Orient Point Hotel, leased the Mount Pleasant House from the Miller family and ran the business for five years. *Courtesy of the Oysterponds Historical Society.*

Mount Pleasant House, Orient, circa 1920. The hotel was run by Jenny Medeiros, John Miller's niece, from 1925 to 1937. The building, situated on the western side of Orient with spectacular views of Orient Harbor and Shelter Island, continued to attract customers when many other hotels were failing. *Courtesy of the Oysterponds Historical Society.*

Advertisement for Mount Pleasant Hotel, Orient, circa 1940. The Mount Pleasant House, which had been renamed the Mount Pleasant Hotel, was purchased in 1937 by William Charlton of Riverhead, who ran the business for three years. In an effort to increase business, he put out this small booklet featuring the modernized charms of the hotel and the Orient area. *Courtesy of the Oysterponds Historical Society.*

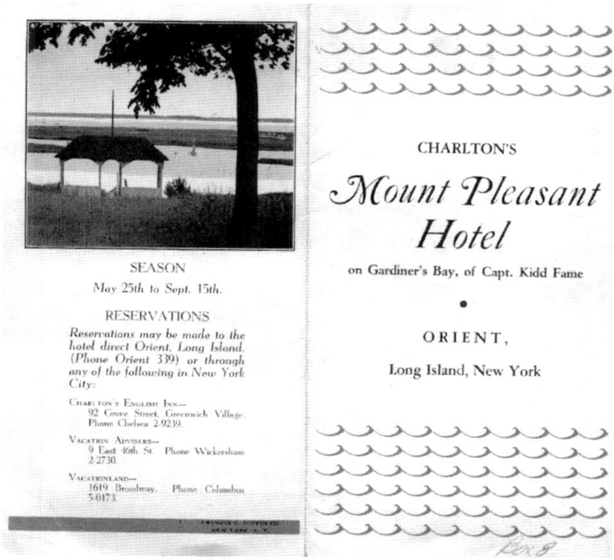

Advertisement for Mount Pleasant Hotel, circa 1940. When the hotel failed to bring in enough guests, Charlton wantonly demolished the building in the late 1940s and divided up the property into house lots. *Courtesy of the Oysterponds Historical Society.*

Guests of a costume party at the Mount Pleasant House, Orient, circa 1935. Costume parties and other entertainments were common and pleasant diversions for guests coming to enjoy the country air. The hotel could offer music performed by its own in-house band. *Courtesy of the Oysterponds Historical Society.*

CHAPTER FOUR

BOARDINGHOUSES

A boardinghouse, also known as a rooming house or lodging house, can be defined as a private home where people could rent a room for as long or as short a time as they needed. Boardinghouses differed from hotels in that guests at a boardinghouse typically would receive a meal as part of the price of the room.

Boardinghouses flourished on the North Fork at the height of the tourist boom at the turn of the century. Multiple boardinghouses existed in most of the North Fork villages that catered to the tourist trade. The large numbers of tourists coming to enjoy the beaches and cooler temperatures each summer spurred many families to take on boarders for the extra income that supplemented their earnings from traditional farming and fishing occupations of the area. A business directory printed in 1910 lists five boardinghouses in Greenport in addition to the eleven hotels in the area.

Many houses accepted long-term guests. Middle-class families would rent rooms for the summer, with the mother and children remaining at the boardinghouses for an extended vacation away from the heat and odors of the city. The fathers would visit the family on their days off from work, traveling back and forth from their jobs in the city by train or boat.

While most boardinghouses attracted visitors from the city, some businesses specialized in catering to a particular type of guest. The Edna Hedges Boarding House rented rooms only to female teachers who were working at the local schools. Another house, Weldnes Boarding House in Greenport, only rented rooms to girls working as maids in the larger hotels.

Many boardinghouses were operated by women. During the nineteenth and early twentieth centuries, women seldom worked outside the home and were expected to give up their jobs or careers when they married. Running a boardinghouse was one of the few occupations that a wife or widow could own and remain respectable.

Many large, older homes that had been built in the mid- to late nineteenth century for the wealthy seeking to rusticate in the country were often converted into boardinghouses catering to the tourist trade. In Orient, the Edward Brothers Boarding House was the former grand home of New York State senator Lewis A. Edwards. South of the Main Road on Village Lane, the Vail home, known locally as Village House, had been expanded to more than double its original size by the family to take advantage of the boom in summer tourists. In Southold, the Albertson House, one of the largest houses in town, was likewise converted into a boardinghouse for the summer trade.

Even with the large number of hotels and boardinghouses on the North Fork, the number of visitors to the area was too great for the supply of rooms.

Locust Grove Hotel, South Jamesport, circa 1900. Built about 1899 by James Downs—brother of Edward Downs, builder of the Great Peconic Bay House—the Locust Grove Hotel was a smaller establishment on the shore slightly east of the larger Great Peconic Bay House. The hotel advertised in the *Brooklyn Eagle* newspaper as having views of two bays and being one hundred feet from Peconic Bay. This establishment competed with Sunnyside House, run by Halsey Corwin, the Bayside House of Benjamin Jones and the Idlewild Hotel run by H. Griffing Downs. *Courtesy of the Cutchogue New Suffolk Library.*

Water Edge Hotel, South Jamesport, circa 1920. The next incarnation of the Locust Grove Hotel was as the Water Edge Hotel. In the 1920s, the building was owned by E.O. Downs and was large enough that it advertised that it could accommodate between seventy-five and eighty-five guests. The building was eventually torn down and the site is now occupied by Motel on the Bay. *Courtesy of the Cutchogue New Suffolk Library.*

Bayview Hotel, South Jamesport, 1941, photograph by Charles Meredith. Owned by John Trages, the hotel was built about the 1840s, and the structure was enlarged over the ensuing decades. At its peak, it held forty guests and advertised in 1920 that its restaurant specialized in seafood home cooking. In 2002, the building was taken over by the same owners as the Motel on the Bay, and it currently operates as the popular Bayview Inn and Restaurant. *Courtesy of the Southold Historical Society.*

Interior of the Bayview Hotel bar and dining room, 1941. *Courtesy of the Southold Historical Society.*

Mattituck Harbor Inn, Mattituck, 1912. The Mattituck Harbor Inn started out as a boardinghouse located on a small peninsula that juts out into Mattituck Harbor. The house was originally built for the Betts family as a vacation home. It was then sold to the I. Gildersleeve family. *Courtesy of Norman Wamback.*

Klein's Harbor Inn, Mattituck, circa 1915. In the late 1800s, the former Betts home was purchased by Dr. Hubert Klein, who was a pharmacist. In 1905, he announced that he was moving his business to his home and he was going to operate a boardinghouse and build a bowling alley for his guests. The Kleins sold the property and business in 1922 to Mrs. Eugenia Sommerman and her sister, Mrs. A. Esposito. *Courtesy of Norman Wamback.*

Klein's Harbor Inn from the water, circa 1906. This view from across Mattituck Harbor shows the small gazebo on the point for guests to admire the view. In 1937, the inn had changed hands again and was owned by M.L. Gardoni of New York City. The devastating hurricane that had blown through in the fall of 1938 did considerable damage to the business by demolishing the bowling alley and garage and uprooting most of the large trees around the property. Gardoni was cleaning up some of the fallen branches from the hurricane when a spark from the fire set the roof of the inn ablaze. The building sustained considerable damage from the fire, which gutted the entire second floor before firefighters were able to extinguish it. The business closed not long afterward. *Courtesy of Norman Wamback.*

Lewis-Cochran House, Southold, circa 1972. Built after 1870, this house stood on the Main Road in Southold. It was owned by Carrie J. Lewis, who used it as a boardinghouse. In 1919, William A. Cochran bought the house, and in 1989 it was sold to developers. The house was demolished and the site is currently occupied by the Feather Hill shopping center. *Courtesy of the Southold Historical Society.*

Spruce Park House, Southold, circa 1900. Built between 1852 and 1856, this impressive Italianate building was operated for a time as a boardinghouse and was owned by Israel Peck, the founder of the Spruce Park racetrack. By the 1880s, both the house and track were renamed "Oaklawn." Located on the Main Road, it had ceased operations as a boardinghouse by 1887. After Peck's death in 1881, the house passed through several owners until it was demolished in 1966. *Courtesy of the Southold Historical Society.*

Albertson House, Southold, circa 1915. Possibly constructed by G.P. Horton, this impressive home was located at the corner of Youngs Avenue and the Main Road in Southold. It was originally the home of William C. and Jennie W. Albertson, and by 1887 the family had opened their residence to boarders. The building was sold in 1899 to W.F. Mitchell, who continued operating the boardinghouse under the name Albertson House. About 1956, the building was demolished to make way for a Bohack supermarket, today's IGA. *Courtesy of the Southold Historical Society.*

Point O' View Inn, Southold, circa 1920. This inn was located on the Main Road in Southold and was built sometime before 1858. The building was originally owned by the Widow Payne. In the early twentieth century, the building was turned into the Point O' View Inn. *Courtesy of the Oysterponds Historical Society.*

Atlantic Manor on the Water, Greenport, circa 1920. This boardinghouse was located on Atlantic Avenue in Greenport, down by Eastern Long Island Hospital (ELIH). It was owned by George E. and Fannie Griffin. George was an oysterman, and when World War II broke out, he enlisted in the navy and died in the war. The boardinghouse closed down around the same time. *Courtesy of the Cutchogue New Suffolk Library.*

Cherry Lane Boarding House, Greenport, circa 1910. The building originally stood on Cherry Lane in Greenport and was operated by Annie Sweezy Benjamin. When her husband, James Benjamin, drowned in 1903, Annie was forced the following year to start taking in boarders to support her children. The Cherry Lane Boarding House did not advertise for guests. All guests had to be recommended. *Collection of Don Boerum.*

Interior of the Benjamin boardinghouse showing the dining room set for guests, circa 1910. *Collection of Don Boerum.*

Pipes Neck House, Greenport, circa 1905. Built in 1823, the original house burned down in 1912 and was rebuilt. It was originally owned by the Corwin family and was located on Peconic Bay on Pipes Neck Road in western Greenport. The boardinghouse was run by Mary (Marie) Holman and her sister, Isadore Judge. Holman was a midwife who also worked as a private home nurse for families all across Greenport, East Marion and Orient. The Pipes Neck House was closed in the 1940s. *Courtesy of the Oysterponds Historical Society.*

Edna and Henry Hedges Boarding House, Greenport, circa 1920. The house was located on Fourth Street in Greenport next to the synagogue. The Hedgeses specialized in renting rooms to female schoolteachers who worked for the Greenport school district. Mrs. Hedges also occasionally served meals as an informal restaurant for people other than her renters. *Courtesy of Edna Terry.*

White Shingles, Orient, circa 1930. Run by local artist Hortense Knox, White Shingles was better known as a tearoom than for its guesthouse. White Shingles boardinghouse consisted of two buildings: one was a guest house with six or seven rooms that could be rented to travelers, and the other was Ms. Knox's residence and the dining area for visitors. The business closed sometime shortly before Ms. Knox's death in 1953. *Courtesy of the Oysterponds Historical Society.*

Brown Boarding House, Orient, circa 1895. This large home was originally built for the Edwin Peter Brown family of Orient. Brown was captain of several whaling ships and traveled all over the world. When he passed away in 1892, his widow, Martha, was forced to start taking in boarders to maintain the house. *Courtesy of the Oysterponds Historical Society.*

Bay House, Orient, circa 1870. The Bay House was originally owned and run by Maria R. Merriman, and the business was known as a temperance hotel. During a time period when most of the larger hotels included a bar among their many attractions, a business that maintained a strict no-alcohol policy was unusual in the summer resort atmosphere that

encompassed most of the North Fork. But fears that alcohol was ruining the health of most of the population were a growing movement that eventually led to Prohibition. *Courtesy of the Oysterponds Historical Society.*

Bay House, Orient, circa 1940. When the original owner, Maria Merriman, passed away in 1896, the business was on the brink of foreclosure when it was purchased at auction by a consortium of local businessmen. Eventually, Cicero Breeze King bought out the other members of the group and owned and operated the Bay House into the 1920s. He and his son, Floyd, and grandson, Floyd Jr., maintained the business as a temperance family hotel until it finally closed in the late 1960s. Today, the Bay House is a private home in Orient. *Courtesy of the Oysterponds Historical Society.*

Bay House Cottages, Orient, circa 1930. Floyd King, who inherited the property from his father, extended the business by renovating the buildings across the street from the Bay House into cottages for rent. The buildings he renovated were formerly C.B. King's meat market and other businesses owned by the family. *Courtesy of the Oysterponds Historical Society.*

Bay House Cottages advertisement, circa 1966. This advertisement for the Bay House was included in a booklet advertising many vacation spots across the North Fork. At this time, Betty (Floyd Jr.'s sister) and her husband, Berg Henriksen, were operating the cottages. *Courtesy of the Southold Historical Society.*

Village House, Orient, circa 1890. This home was originally built in the 1820s by Augustus Griffin, a historian, writer, general storekeeper and innkeeper in Orient. The home was purchased by Samuel G. Vail in 1853 and inherited and expanded by Jeremiah Vail in the 1880s. Samuel's wife, Roxanna, ran the building as a boardinghouse, and her daughter-in-law, Nancy, continued the business after her husband inherited the property. Today, the Village House is part of the Oysterponds Historical Society and is being restored to show the heyday of the turn-of-the-century summer boardinghouse trade on the North Fork. *Courtesy of the Oysterponds Historical Society.*

Advertising card for the Village House, Orient, circa 1870–80. The Village House must have had a loyal and repeat clientele, because it seldom advertised. This card is one of the few advertisements known to exist. *Courtesy of the Oysterponds Historical Society.*

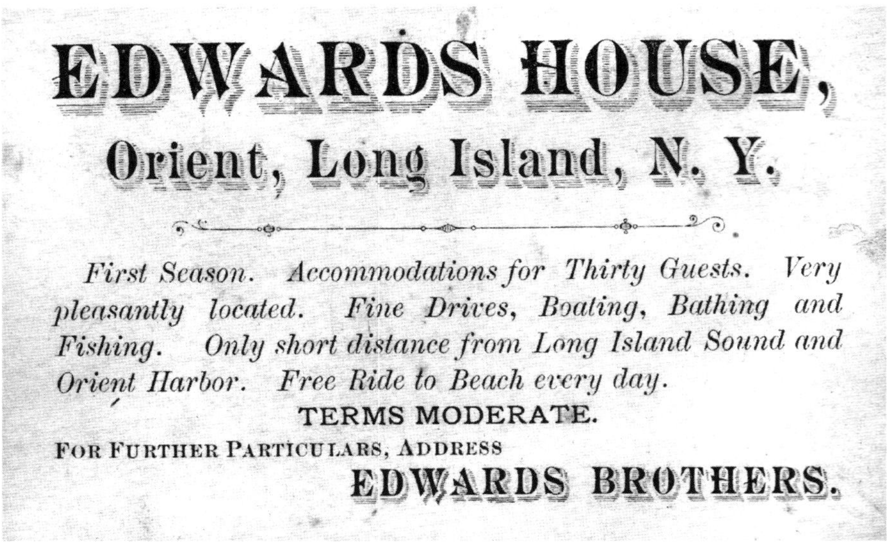

Edwards Brothers House advertising card, Orient, circa 1880. The impressive Second Empire building that served as the Edwards House was originally built by Lewis Edwards, who served as the New York State senator for the East End of Long Island. He was involved in many business ventures in the area, including the local menhaden fish-processing plant in Orient. The house was purchased by Lewis's brother John, who turned the house into the Edward Bros. House in 1869. The hand card advertised that it could accommodate thirty guests. *Courtesy of the Oysterponds Historical Society.*

Edwards Brothers House, Orient, circa 1900. John Edwards, who had converted the home into a boardinghouse, left the business to his wife to manage as he traveled overseas. In 1876, he died of yellow fever in Brazil, and his widow lost the house a year later to foreclosure. The new owners renamed it the Seward House and continued operating the boardinghouse until 1886, when the house was converted back into a summer mansion for the Dyer family. During the 1930s and '40s, the building became the Buttonwood Inn, a tearoom catering to automobile travelers heading for Orient Point. Today, the house is once again a private home. *Courtesy of the Oysterponds Historical Society.*

Hommel House, Orient, circa 1910. Just down the street from Village House and next door to the Bay House in Orient, the Hommel House was a small boardinghouse near the foot of the Orient Wharf. "Gus" Hommel owned a small shoe store next to the house, which in 1894 caught fire and burned to the ground with the Youngs Meat Market next door. The residents of Orient who were not fighting the fire helped the family to move most of the contents of the house out into the street when the building seemed in danger of burning. The house was ruined from the intense heat and the water damage, but it was rebuilt and was back in operation by 1895. *Courtesy of the Oysterponds Historical Society.*

Hommel House, Orient, circa 1900. A traveler enjoys a nap in the Hommel House hammock while another friend has climbed the tree at right. The boardinghouse closed down in the 1920s when Gus and his wife passed away. Today, the building is a private residence. *Courtesy of the Oysterponds Historical Society.*

CHAPTER FIVE

RESORTS

Other than singular hotels and boardinghouses, there was another form that buildings constructed for the hospitality industry could take: resorts. The primary difference between these sites and others was the inclusion of (1) a grand hotel, (2) bountiful amenities and (3) separate, independent cottages that could be rented by the week or month or purchased outright. These resorts were in fact a way to encourage more independent-minded individuals, as well as families, to come to the North Fork to vacation. Those visitors staying in a resort could operate on their own schedule, prepare their own meals if they wished to and could rely on the induced separation to avoid other guests if they so wished. Most of these resorts appeared in the early twentieth century and nearly all were gone by the 1940s.

Resorts were uncommon on the North Fork—most hotel operators preferred to keep all aspects of operation within a single building. It was not only more efficient to offer services this way, but it was also cheaper. They did not have to build, furnish or maintain separate structures that had their own inherent problems (leaky roofs, water problems, additional staffing, etc.).

Though all hotels, inns and boardinghouses had some sort of social activities, such as balls, dances or picnics, resorts offered a much wider array of services. Hunting and fishing parties, golf outings, boat rentals and transportation to other locales were some of the amenities that grew up around the resorts.

In later years, simple cottage resorts would replace those that included larger, more lavish hotels. They would be "efficiency"-style locations offering the opposite of what the grander resorts had once offered—just the most basic accommodations. The automobile made it possible for guests to wander on their own and find things to do. These smaller, simpler locations would be the immediate predecessor of an American icon—the motel.

Opposite, top: Peconic Park Hotel, Nassau Point, 1883. This enormous hotel was part of a massive resort planned for Nassau Point, located between Cutchogue and Peconic, named "Peconic Park." It was to have its own Long Island Rail Road spur from Peconic to take guests directly to the Point, where they would be able to enjoy many different types of amenities, including bathing, sailing and horseback riding. The promoters hired noted American artist Harry Fenn (1845–1911) to illustrate the lavish proposal prospectus they distributed. Had it been built, it would have accommodated several hundred guests. But the promoters' grand plans for Nassau Point came to nothing and the massive hotel was never constructed. *Courtesy of the Southold Historical Society.*

Opposite, bottom: The Burr Mansion, Nassau Point, circa 1918. The entire spit of land today known as Nassau Point was originally named "Little Hog Neck." By the 1850s, Brooklyn investors Edward White Burr (b. 1813) and John Carrington (his wife's uncle) acquired all of the Neck for the then princely sum of $6,000, renaming it "Mattawauk." Eventually, Carrington acquired sole title (after the bankruptcy of Burr in 1871–72) to the approximately five hundred acres on Nassau Point and sold it, in 1872, to a Mr. Wilson, who after many false starts, later proposed the erection of the massive hotel and resort known as "Peconic Park." This project failed, and by 1903 the property had been sold to investors in New York City. *Courtesy of the Southold Historical Society.*

Proposed Hotel.

The Nassau Point Clubhouse and Hotel, Nassau Point, circa 1925. The Burr Mansion, greatly enlarged by Mr. Wilson, was converted into a clubhouse and hotel for people who bought land and built homes on the newly named "Nassau Point." The already existing bowling alley and tennis courts were rebuilt and refurbished, and the reputation of the food at the club grew to a point where the local press noted, "Their reputation for savory meals extends throughout the East End." In 1924, the clubhouse was greatly enlarged and redecorated, including the addition of a third floor and seventeen more guestrooms at a cost of over $35,000. The hotel, which had been more of a burden than an asset, looked like it would finally begin to act as the latter. But it was not to be. On June 18, 1928, with the hotel fully booked for the upcoming season, the building was destroyed by fire—eliminating forever one of the most elegant holiday facilities on the North Fork. *Courtesy of the Southold Historical Society.*

Opposite, top: The Paumonok Inn, Southold, circa 1910. The Paumonok was one of the first great resort hotels built on the North Fork. The original portion of the building had been the old Southold Union School. After its closure, the largest part of the school was purchased by George F. Hummel and rolled up to Horton's Point and enlarged into the hotel. As manager, Hummel promoted the hotel widely, creating cleverly crafted brochures that advertised the "never-failing sea breeze" that swept past the hotel. *Courtesy of the Southold Historical Society.*

Opposite, bottom: The Paumonok Inn, Southold, circa 1912. The inn was located on a beautiful piece of land adjacent to the Horton Point Lighthouse, which was built in 1857. The lighthouse may have bothered guests, as it does some neighbors today. Its bright light shines strongly at night, prompting some nearby residents in the past to ask for the light to be turned off at night. Here, guests stroll the lawn of the inn while one gentleman plays a little golf. *Courtesy of the Southold Historical Society*

May 30th to October 1st

Paumonok Inn

HORTON'S POINT
SOUTHOLD, L. I.

Situated on the crest of the 100 foot Cliff, directly overlooking Long Island Sound, and swept from north and south by the never-failing sea breeze.

Geo. F. Hummel, Manager

The Cottage Colony at the Paumonok, Southold, 1913. Not long after opening, cottages were introduced up at the Point. The cottages were constructed on a thirty-acre lot surrounding the hotel, and as one brochure noted, "can be purchased for the amount of rental paid for a summer cottage." Artistically designed, most cottages averaged six to seven rooms and were equipped with "bath, gas, [and] rough-stone fireplaces." Part of the advantage of acquiring a house was membership in the Paumonok Club, the benefits of which included the management of houses when closed for the season, access to tennis courts and discounted rates at the hotel. *Courtesy of the Southold Historical Society.*

The Russell Cottage, Southold, 1913. This image shows a good example of a cottage at the colony belonging to the Russell family. Simple, shingle-style structures incorporating rough stone appear to have been popular with those investing in the colony property. By 1913, the hotel had left the hands of George Hummel and was being operated and managed by W.J. Palmer of 108 Fulton Street, New York City. *Courtesy of the Southold Historical Society.*

Brochure, 1913. W.J. Palmer produced an elegant brochure for the 1913 season, which introduced the reader to all the amenities that were available during a given season. He noted in the brochure that the "Inn has been thoroughly renovated this spring and equipped with modern improvements, including the addition of many private baths." *Courtesy of the Southold Historical Society.*

"Paumonok Doings," 1913. Palmer included a sampling of activities—from fishing to hunting—that could be enjoyed at the inn. This grouping of images highlights just a few of the available entertainments that the hotel provided. He also advertised a captain who could aid fishermen as well as those just interested in "many a nautical tale." *Courtesy of the Southold Historical Society.*

Sound View House, Southold, circa 1917. A few years later, the Paumonok Inn changed its name to the Sound View House and again later to the Horton Point Hotel. The hotel and colony never became all that successful, and by the 1920s had ceased operation. One reason may have been World War I, which caused a fairly severe drop in visitation to the North Fork. The hotel building itself no longer exists, though many of the cottage colony structures survive and have been converted to year-round residences. *Courtesy of the Southold Historical Society.*

Arshamomaque Inn, Beixedon, circa 1925. In the case of the Arshamomaque Inn, it was a wealthy Brooklynite who decided to get into the resort business. Shown here in its early days, the inn was located on the bay side of Southold. The inn was owned and developed by Bennet De Beixedon (1889–1935), scion of a wealthy French-American family and grandson of George C. Bennet, founder of the *Brooklyn Times*. The Arshamomaque Inn was opened for business in June 1921 and quickly became a popular summer resort. *Courtesy of the Southold Historical Society.*

The Beixedon Beach, 1936. Bennet De Beixedon saw the possibilities in Southold, and also developed Beixedon Cottages, a summer colony not unlike the one that was created around the Paumonok Inn. The colony included many houses designed in a variety of styles, which were available for rental during the summer months. Many of these summer cottages still exist today. During the time of De Beixedon's ownership, the official name of the resort was the Arshamomaque Inn and Cottages. Behind the group relaxing on the beach is the cottage named "the Cedar." *Courtesy of Joan Latham.*

A Beixedon cottage, "the Orchard," 1936. The houses built as part of the cottage colony were not only different stylistically, but were also of different sizes, allowing the consumer to choose the one that would best suit his/her situation. Cottages were offered fully furnished, and could be rented either for the full season or a half season, which began August 1. Prices ranged from $350 to $600 per house, depending on the size and location. Residents could eat at the hotel and could be furnished (at a slight charge) with maid service to take care of any housework needed during their stay. Shown here are Joan and Marie Williams in front of the family cottage at Beixedon, "the Orchard." *Courtesy of Joan Latham.*

After the fire, 1940s. Just twenty years after being built, in July 1941, the Arshamomaque Inn was destroyed by fire. De Beixedon, having died several years before, left a wave of debt that could not be overcome by his widow, Grace. In 1946, many of the remaining cottages were sold at auction by Joseph Day of New York City. Today, the former colony is now known as Beixedon Estates, a private community located in Southold. *Courtesy of Joan Latham.*

Mansion House, Fishers Island, circa 1906. Though located closer to Connecticut, Fishers Island is part of Southold Town. The Mansion House was originally the home of the Winthrop family and was built in 1882. The home was purchased by the Ferguson brothers in 1889, and the hotel was opened for business in 1892. It was expanded several times until, by 1910, the hotel boasted that it was able to accommodate two hundred guests in the main building, with another thirty cottages that could hold one hundred visitors. The hotel closed down in 1941 and was partially demolished. The only section that remains today is the original Winthrop home. *Courtesy of the Southold Historical Society.*

Mansion House, Fishers Island, circa 1900. A view down the drive leading up to the hotel. The building screened by the trees was situated at the west end of the island, close to the other large hotels constructed nearby. *Courtesy of the Southold Historical Society.*

Mononotto Hotel, Fishers Island, circa 1916. This grand structure was built by Maria Hoppes and family of Bethlehem, Pennsylvania. The inn was constructed between 1892 and 1893 and was enlarged in 1894. It could hold 175 guests at its peak and remained in business until 1930. The building was torn down in 1939. The inn advertised two barrooms, two orchestras, two ballrooms, a beauty parlor, a barbershop and availability of a tailor for guests. The Fishers Island hotels were luxury resorts that catered to the wealthy and

were not known for their equal treatment of people, especially people who were not from their social circle. In 1912, Julius Tannenbaum, a respected captain in the New York State National Guard, was asked to leave the hotel because he was Jewish. *Courtesy of the Southold Historical Society*.

Munnatawket Hotel, Fishers Island, circa 1910. The Munnatawket was originally the Lyles Beach Hotel. Standing on the western end of Fishers Island, the building was owned and operated by the Ferguson brothers. It was given the name Munnatawket, which was the Indian name for the island. This hotel was the smallest of the Fishers Island hotels in that it could only hold 150 guests. The building was renovated and downsized in 1905 and then re-expanded in 1912. It was torn down in 1926 after it fell into disrepair. *Courtesy of the Southold Historical Society.*

Silvermere Bungalows, Greenport, circa 1930, and Silvermere advertisement, 1960s. A smaller type of resort, Silvermere Bungalows was located on the bay between Southold and Greenport. In the 1960s, the bungalows were expanded to include the Silver Sands Motel. The bungalows were the precursor to the many motels that would develop in the decades following World War II. *Courtesy of the Cutchogue New Suffolk Library.*

Pleasant View Cottages and Windward Shore advertisements, 1960s. Like Silvermere Bungalows, these two small resorts offered independently occupied cottages and other amenities, such as access to golf courses, outdoor grills and private beaches. Both were located in Greenport. While Windward Shore no longer operates under that name, Pleasant View Cottages still offers "four beautiful waterfront cottages" for rent during the summer. *Courtesy of the Southold Historical Society.*

CHAPTER SIX

RUMRUNNING AND HOUSES OF ILL REPUTE

Once the 1919 Volstead Act eliminated the production and sale of alcoholic beverages in the United States, the process of violating that act began. From subtly hidden speakeasies to the trafficking of all types of liquor and spirits, this became the age of rumrunning.

The average person today would find it hard to believe that the North Fork, which is now so family oriented, was once one of the largest entry points for the distribution of illegal alcohol in the country (along with the Jersey Shore). Residents of Greenport played an important role in the transportation and distribution of illegal liquor. It was noted by local historian Lois Swaney in her paper "Prohibition—1920–1933, A Review of Enriching Local Activities during the 'Noble Experiment,'" that "most of the population of Greenport in the 1920's derived some form of profit from their disregard of the Prohibition Law." The U.S. Coast Guard, which was charged with defeating the rumrunners, actively patrolled the Long Island shore in hopes of capturing a liquor-loaded prize. On several occasions, this led to all-out chases and even gun battles.

In addition to rumrunning, the other activity that became nearly as profitable was the establishment and management of "houses of ill repute." Prostitution was linked with the liquor trade, and the North Fork of Long Island became a center for both illicit activities. The buildings and structures used for prostitution-related purposes were wide and varied, and included many hotels and inns. Stories help identify some, while others today no longer exist. One very successful speakeasy and house of prostitution was the Pastime Inn, located in Peconic on the northwest corner of Mill Lane and the North Road (also known as Route 48). Girls from New York City would unload from the LIRR on Friday nights and head over to the Pastime to work the men. The large building burned down in a spectacular fire about 1938. Many people made a living off of these industries. One local resident recalled as a young boy that he carried bags for one of the most notorious madams, "Madam Pam," who operated out of Greenport.

It has to be understood that local police were nearly always involved in some manner in both of these activities, even if it was only by looking the other way. There are many stories concerning Pat Kelly, the first uniformed police officer in Southold Town. The one that makes people smile the most is the tale of how he buried tons of silver coins around his property—all of which were supposedly part of the payoffs he received from rumrunners. At one point Kelly got caught with a stash of illegal liquor on his property and lost his job, but he was quickly reinstated through the efforts of his compatriots.

In those days, Greenport village had its own police force, and it was all too happy to see the likes of Madam Pam open up shop. The reason behind this was simple—it was a time when the fishing industry in the village was booming and many young men came to work on what were called "bunker boats." After a hard day's work, all these young men had nothing to do, and many fights ensued in the village. The establishment of Madam Pam and her like did two things: one, it kept the boys busy and out of trouble when they were not on the boats; and two, the money the ladies took from the boys' paychecks was inevitably put right back into the community during those tough times. At least one resident, Dr. J. Mott Heath, received compensation from them—he was a prominent physician and is known to have looked after the medical needs of Madam Pam's many female employees. Her influence could even be felt in death when Town Supervisor Albert Martoccia gave the eulogy at her funeral.

Madam Pam was not alone, however. While she mainly managed the African American market in Greenport, her chief competitor, the "Madam in the Black Veil," catered to the white population. The "Madam in the Black Veil" was in fact a local woman named Dorothy Conklin. Her trademark black veil was used to hide the disfiguring deformations that were evident on her face, caused by untreated tertiary syphilis. Her large Victorian house, once located on the corner of Front Street and Railroad Avenue, was a haven for those interested in "ladies of the night." Other service providers included "One-Armed Len," who had his own taxi service in addition to his own brothel.

Activities like rumrunning and prostitution helped villages like Greenport and others weather the depression years, as both industries required extensive manpower and, in the case of rumrunning, boats. This again is evident in Lois Swaney's research, where she stated that on one occasion "a local Southold citizen counted 76 rum-runners in the Greenport harbor at the same time." Favorite landing spots in Southold Town included Cedar Beach, Reydon Shores and out at Paradise Point, both located on Great Hog Neck in the area known today as Bayview.

While rumrunning would end with the collapse of Prohibition in 1933, prostitution was not something that was so easily erased from the North Fork. It would linger for a period following the end of the "noble experiment."

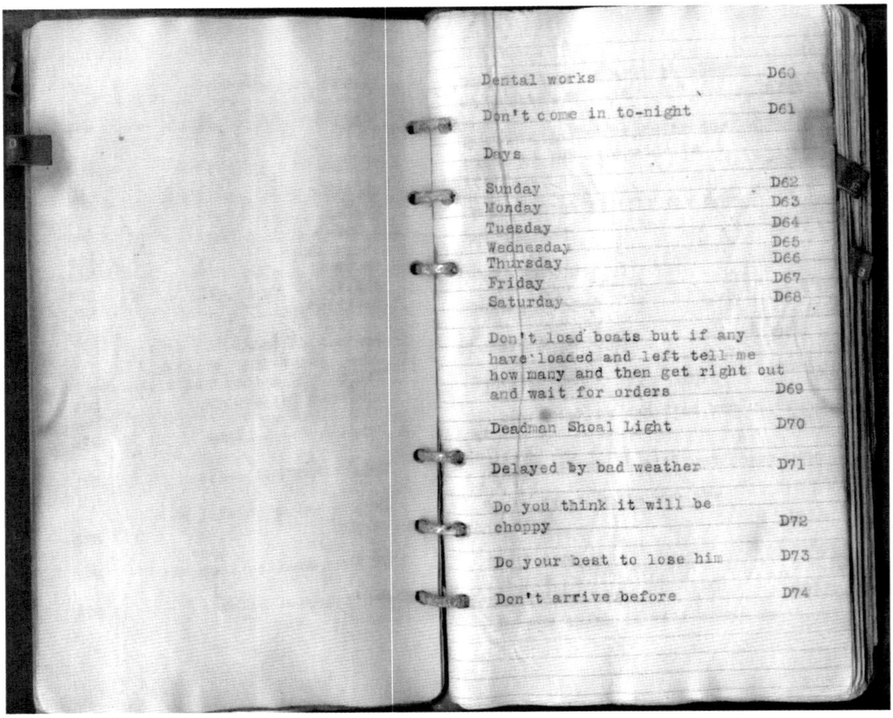

Dental works D60

Don't come in to-night D61

Days

Sunday D62
Monday D63
Tuesday D64
Wednesday D65
Thursday D66
Friday D67
Saturday D68

Don't load boats but if any have loaded and left tell me how many and then get right out and wait for orders D69

Deadman Shoal Light D70

Delayed by bad weather D71

Do you think it will be choppy D72

Do your best to lose him D73

Don't arrive before D74

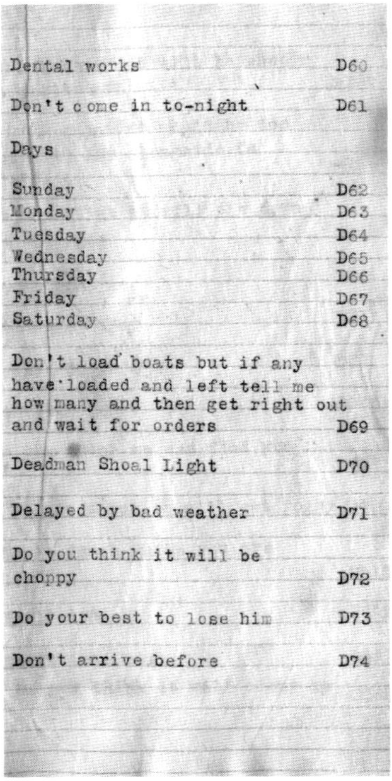

Dental works D60

Don't come in to-night D61

Days

Sunday D62
Monday D63
Tuesday D64
Wednesday D65
Thursday D66
Friday D67
Saturday D68

Don't load boats but if any have loaded and left tell me how many and then get right out and wait for orders D69

Deadman Shoal Light D70

Delayed by bad weather D71

Do you think it will be choppy D72

Do your best to lose him D73

Don't arrive before D74

Above: Rumrunners codebook, circa 1930. To evade the authorities, rumrunners needed a system of codes that could be easily understood by their various contingents. However, due to the number of codes needed, it would only be easy if they had their codebook handy. This codebook, thrown from a rumrunner off eastern Long Island during a chase in the early 1930s, is a rare survivor from the period. *Courtesy of the Oysterponds Historical Society.*

Left: Rumrunners codebook, detail, circa 1930. Exactly how such a codebook would be used is difficult to determine. Each day of the week had a code, as did different activities involved in the transporting and delivery of goods. Locations were also detailed, as were the various codes for different international locations—from Scotland (where a good deal of liquor came from) to the United States. *Courtesy of the Oysterponds Historical Society.*

This page: The Old Mill Inn, Mattituck, circa 1910. The Old Mill, constructed in Mattituck in 1821, had at one time been a place of industrial business. When milling days came to an end in 1902, the mill was sold and turned into a tavern. During the Prohibition era, it was an isolated spot from which illegal spirits could be had. Captain Stanley Naugles operated the inn along with his brother. Naugles helped out the local rumrunners by using his plane to warn them of impending revenuers. The addition of two guestrooms has led many to speculate that it may also have doubled as a place where "ladies of the night" could take paying customers. Today, the traditional hospitality of the North Fork is preserved at the Old Mill, one of the longest operating bars and restaurants on eastern Long Island. *Courtesy of the Southold Historical Society.*

Bill
BERTHA.

Interior, the Old Mill, Mattituck, 1940. The great hand-hewn beams of the old mill are easily identifiable in this image. It became the habit for regulars and visitors alike to "make their mark" upon the old beams to record their visits, whether they be long or short. The fireplace was an addition to the building, built after 1910. *Courtesy of the Southold Historical Society.*

Worthwhile Lodge, Peconic, circa 1940s. The Worthwhile Lodge was located on Mill Road near where the old Peconic tidal mill had once stood. A notorious speakeasy, there was a fine dance hall located upstairs, while liquor was hidden in a dredged-out spot in the water of Goldsmith Inlet below. This once notable structure had come down by the 1960s. *Courtesy of Southold Free Library.*

Opposite, top: Lake Lodge, Peconic, 1949. What began as a popular social facility would turn into a favorite haunt of both rumrunners and those seeking a bit of "extracurricular" activity. The building began its life as the structure at left, with the addition of a large bar and hall at the right rear. A popular spot, it was later "cleaned up" and operated by the Polish-American Independent Club of Southold, which was founded in 1936. The club held many social events there, including its New Year's Eve Ball in 1939. *Courtesy of the Southold Historical Society.*

Opposite, bottom: Lake Lodge interior, Peconic, 1949. The Polish-American Independent Club expanded Lake Lodge to accommodate a growing membership, its numbers swelling to several hundred members. The rough hewn timbers and simulated bamboo–covered bar were popular decorative motifs of the period. Today, Lake Lodge is preserved as a private home. *Courtesy of the Southold Historical Society.*

Meredith
Sept-24-1949

Claudio's, Greenport, circa 1910. Claudio's became a great haven for rumrunning activities during the Prohibition era. It had a novel feature that was not available to everyone else—a trapdoor below the building where boats could park and unload their illegal goods in secret. Like so many speakeasies of the period, there were good days

and bad days. In April 1924, a massive cargo of illicit liquor was captured on land between Orient and Greenport, consisting of 560 cases valued at over $28,000. A neighboring speakeasy near Claudio's, named Jo-Jo's, was filled with a grieving crowd that night! *Courtesy of the Southold Historical Society.*

The Docia House, Greenport, circa 1930s. Dorothy Conklin, who was known as the "Madam in the Black Veil," operated out of this grand Victorian residence located at the corner of Front and Third Street. Her personal nickname was "Docia," hence the name of the house. Later the building was divided into apartments, and today the site is occupied by the Bridgehampton National Bank building. *Courtesy of the Oysterponds Historical Society.*

Opposite, top: The big guns, circa 1928. Not all Coast Guard ships were small or swift. This image depicts the Coast Guard destroyer USS *Tucker*, which became the flagship of the Coast Guard's Prohibition forces based out of New London, Connecticut. It was originally commissioned in 1916, part of the improved warships that would soon be needed during American participation in World War I. During the war, it saw service off the British Isles and the coast of France. *Tucker* would serve as part of the Coast Guard fleet from 1926 to 1933. *Courtesy of the United States Coast Guard.*

Opposite, middle: Offloading the *Katherine*, circa 1930s. The rumrunning supply ships would lie off the coast and await the visit of rumrunners in smaller boats, who then could race to shore with their illegal stock. Here the British schooner *Katherine* prepares to load some of its illicit cargo aboard a small motorboat that has arrived near its mooring place off the New Jersey coast. To hide their move to shore, boats most often traveled under the cover of darkness. Rumrunners also employed other tactics to evade the authorities. On the North Fork, at least one seaplane would fly as a lookout to watch for Coast Guard ships. *Courtesy of the United States Coast Guard.*

Opposite, bottom: Caught, 1925. The Coast Guard also made use of seaplanes, and here they have found a prize: the schooner *Almeida*, of Newfoundland, photographed off the Long Island coast in May 1925. Its fully loaded decks, filled with endless bottles of liquor, are clearly visible. *Courtesy of the United States Coast Guard.*

CG-23

Coast Guard boats at the ready, circa 1930. The Coast Guard had many vessels at its disposal, but none quite so popular as the 75- and 125-foot patrol boats. While the 75-foot boats tended to be used for general Prohibition enforcement, the 125-footers, called "Buck and a Quarters," were used primarily for operations that took place farther out at sea. One of their primary duties was the trailing of rumrunning supply ships (called mother ships) that remained just beyond the territorial waters of the United States to avoid capture. *Courtesy of the United States Coast Guard.*

Filled to the brim, 1924. Seizure was always the goal when chasing or hunting the rumrunning vessels and their supply ships. In this image, the heavily crowded decks of the ship *Kirk and Sweeney* are shown not long after its capture by the Coast Guard. The ship was put to use by the Coast Guard after its capture—it became the USS *Chase*, a training vessel for the Coast Guard Academy. For rumrunners working on eastern Long Island, 1924 was a bad year, with hundreds of cases of liquor captured by authorities. *Courtesy of the United States Coast Guard.*

The USCGC *Seneca*, circa 1930. Commissioned in 1908 as a "derelict destroyer," its purpose was to seek out and destroy abandoned wrecks that were still afloat and that might be dangerous to other vessels. After 1922, it joined the hunt for those violating Prohibition laws. Its greatest capture was the ship *Tomoka*, a notorious rumrunner, off the western tip of Long Island in 1923. After a spirited chase, which included the firing of shells across its bow, the *Tomoka* surrendered and was taken off to Staten Island. *Courtesy of the United States Coast Guard.*

CHAPTER SEVEN

MOTELS

As the automobile became more popular, it gave the American middle-class families more freedom to travel the countryside. Instead of being tied to one location for vacation, families could visit parts of the country not serviced by the railroad or steamship. While some early cars came equipped with tents, for those not interested in camping, the new style of hotel came into being.

The modern descendant of the hotels and boardinghouses of the past was the motel, which began appearing as early as the 1930s in America. The word "motel" was first used in California and was a contraction of the words "motor" and "hotel." Not as fancy as a hotel or as restrictive as living in a boardinghouse, the motel blended self-service casualness with economical cost and temporary quarters.

The motel appealed to families for several reasons. Generally built in long, low rows, the motel allowed guests to drive their cars (and luggage) right up to the front door of their room. Guests could bring their belongings to their rooms themselves, with no bellhops to tip. Since most early motels didn't have formal dining rooms, bars or parlors, there were no dress codes for guests. Most motels had more child-friendly activities, such as miniature golf or swimming pools, than many hotels or boardinghouses.

Motels were seldom located in the downtown areas; instead, they were located just outside or, in the case of Long Island, in between different village jurisdictions. Properties that could accommodate the sprawling architecture that defines most motels was not available in most downtown areas, and the advantages of being just outside the local restrictions helped motels develop their own quirky styles.

While few in number, motels started appearing on the East End just after World War II. The booming tourist trade from New York City was a thing of the past, and many of the large hotels and boardinghouses had gone out of business with the advent of World War I. After the war, the Great Depression put the nail in the coffin of the tourist trade on Long Island.

The modern traveler was looking for more than peace and relaxation for vacation. While the East End offered beautiful views and a multitude of water sports, it was too far for the average city traveler. Robert Moses built parkways for city dwellers to escape the heat of the city, but they only had to travel as far as Jones Beach in Nassau County, or for the truly adventurous, the Southern State Parkway would take them as far as Heckscher State Park in Suffolk County. The Long Island Expressway did not extend out to Riverhead until 1973, and until then travelers had to use local roads to reach the East End. The few who came as far as the North Fork could find one motel in Mattituck, one motel in Cutchogue and a small cluster of motels on the west side of Greenport.

Among the many motels that have disappeared or are no longer operating are such businesses as the Victoria Motel, Cozee Cove and Dan Brown's Cabins.

Sunset Motel, Greenport, circa 1960. Perched on the cliffs above Long Island Sound, the Sunset Motel was built by the Molin brothers. The business was eventually taken over by Vera Molin until 1977, when she retired. The property was sold to Donna Levin. In 2001, the motel was taken over by her daughter, Ellen, and is currently run by Donna Levin's granddaughter, Martha. The Sunset Motel is the sister business to the Soundview Motel. *Courtesy of the Cutchogue New Suffolk Library.*

Drossos Motel, Greenport, circa 1966. The business started out as a bed-and-breakfast-style of inn by the Drossos family, and during the 1960s it was rebuilt in the more modern motel style with a miniature golf course. In 1963, the main unit of the hotel—a three-story, sixteen-room building that had formerly been a tavern called the Half Way House—burned down in a huge fire on New Year's Day. *Courtesy of the Southold Historical Society.*

Silver Sands Motel, Greenport, circa 1965. Still in operation today, the Silver Sands Motel is located on Peconic Bay just to the west of Greenport. This motel has been in operation since about 1958. This one-story motel was constructed in a classic U shape. The motel's central court opens out toward the beach, and its site possesses one of the finest views of Peconic Bay. *Courtesy of the Southold Historical Society.*

This page: Southold Town Beach Motel, 1961. Located in between Long Island Sound and Hashamomuck Pond, the town beach is situated on the land where, during the American Revolution, the whaleboat raiders under the command of Jonathan Meigs from Connecticut pulled their boats across the narrow strip of land on their way to the South Fork to capture British soldiers. Built by Helmut Haas circa 1955, the motel changed its name to Southold Beach Motel when the Town of Southold requested that the business not include the word "Town" in its name. This motel was originally constructed with its own pier where boat travelers could dock. In 2005, the motel changed hands, and today it is run by Amy Uyanik. *Courtesy of the Southold Historical Society.*

North Fork Motel under construction, Southold, 1965. This picture was taken by Charles Meredith, a photographer who documented much of the mid-twentieth-century changes in Southold Town. The motel was built by the Laakso brothers of Rockville Center. It was a forty-three-unit, two-story building designed in a sharp V shape that maximized the water view for all of the rooms. The motel also featured a modern luncheonette and swimming pool. *Courtesy of the Southold Historical Society.*

North Fork Motel, Southold, circa 1970. The North Fork Motel was built diagonally across the street from the Southold Beach Motel and just west of Southold Town Beach. Today, this two-story motel has been converted into condominiums. *Courtesy of the Southold Historical Society.*

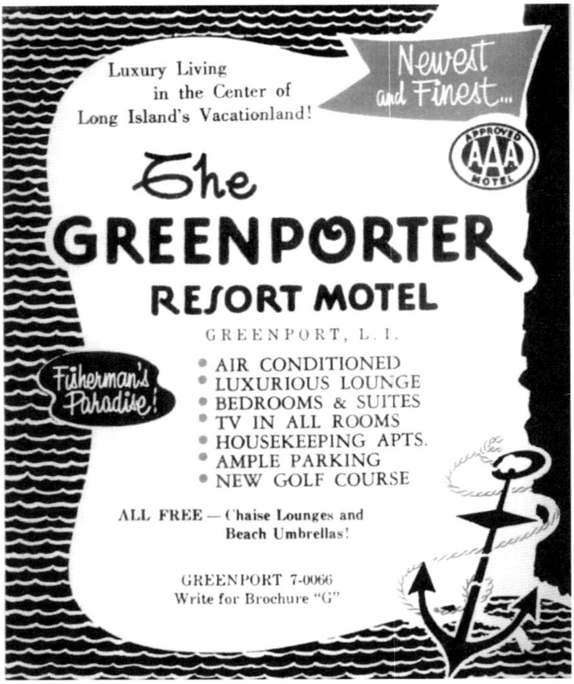

This page and opposite, top: Greenporter Motel, Greenport, images and ad circa 1960–75. The only motel built in the city of Greenport during the 1950s, the Greenporter displays classic mid-century architecture. The motel was built by Jack Levin, who was originally from the Greenport area, about 1957. It was owned and run by the Levin family until 2000, when it was sold to Debra Rivera. *Courtesy of the Cutchogue New Suffolk Library.*

Advertisement for the Motel on the Bay, South Jamesport, circa 1960. Located in South Jamesport, the Motel on the Bay is situated on the former site of the Waters Edge Hotel. The older section of the building started out as the laundry/washhouse/servant quarters for the Great Peconic Bay House. *Courtesy of the Southold Historical Society.*

Mattituck Motel, Mattituck, circa 1960. Tucked in a quiet side street off the Main Road, the Mattituck Motel is one of the few motels on the North Fork outside of Greenport. This motel started out during the 1890s as the Bay View Cottages owned by Mrs. Bicking, whose husband was a barber. The cottages were created from reused structures from the surrounding neighborhood. The Bickings sold the business to Bessie Gaffney, who changed the business to the Gaffney Cottages and then closed it after a year. By the 1950s, the cottages were operating as the Mattituck Motel and had been modernized and moved together to form a more classic motel-style building. The motel frequently played host to the New York Yankees baseball team members who would come out to fish. In 1960, Emilie Haunstetter owned the business and advertised the motel as having apartments and overnight rooms as well as a large recreation facility for guests. Currently, the motel is run by Kerry Navarra. *Courtesy of Kerry Navarra.*

Motel

This page and opposite: Sound Shore Resort Motel, Greenport, circa 1970s. Now more familiarly known as the Soundview Motel and Restaurant, the motel was opened for business by Jack and Irving Levin in 1952, under the name Sound Shore Resort Motel. From the mid-1950s until 1964, the motel expanded in stages. In 1959, the motel was selected to be featured in a Comet cleanser advertisement. Next to the motel was a business named the Soundview Restaurant. About 1967, Jack Levin purchased the restaurant and changed the name of the motel complex to the Soundview Motel. Today, his children continue to operate the business. *Courtesy of Ellen Levin and the Southold Historical Society.*

CHAPTER EIGHT

Bed-and-Breakfasts

The most recent addition to the types of accommodations available on the North Fork of Long Island is the bed-and-breakfast, nearly always abbreviated as B&B. They have become a predominant choice for those of middle- and upper middle–class means as motels have fallen out of favor, seeming old-fashioned and often out of step with their more modern values. The B&Bs are the luxurious reinvention of the boardinghouse.

In the simplest terms, B&Bs offer a bed for the night and breakfast in the morning, most often without offering any additional meals to guests. They have traditionally been operated by families and individuals who have rooms to spare and also want to supplement their incomes. Owners usually occupy the same house used for their B&B, though in some locations that is not required. Many are housed in historic homes, adding to the charm of staying in one. B&Bs in the United States are fairly heavily regulated and they have formed their own local, regional and national trade groups to represent their interests.

Bed-and-breakfasts were not an American invention as some may think. They have a history that dates back to the earliest periods of recorded history. In early times, many European monasteries offered accommodation in the same manner that many B&Bs do today. The United States, as one source notes, "also has a history of bed and breakfasts dating back to the time of early settlers. As the pioneers traveled the trails and roads across this county, they sought a safe refuge in homes, inns and taverns. In fact, some of those historic accommodations now serve as B&Bs."

But it was in Europe, in the United Kingdom, that the term originated. In other countries, a variety of local expressions is used to describe the services provided by a typical B&B in the United Kingdom and North America. B&Bs in the United States owe much to their counterparts in Europe, which served as the original model for the American B&B. According to one researcher for the Wikipedia entry on the subject, it all harkens back to the period just following World War II,

> *middle-class Americans began traveling in Europe in large numbers, many experiencing the European-style B&Bs (Zimmer frei in Germany, chambres d'hotes in France) for the first time. Some were inspired to open B&Bs in the U.S.; tourist home owners updated their properties as B&Bs. The interest in B&Bs coincided with an increasing interest in historic preservation, spurred by the U.S. Bicentennial in 1976 and assisted by two crucial pieces of legislation: the National Historic Preservation Act of 1966, and the Tax Reform Act of 1976, which provided tax incentives for the restoration and reuse of historic structures.*

Today, due to the exposure and interest that the Internet and worldwide web allow, B&Bs are growing both in number and also in popularity. They can be found in every state and community—from bustling cities to the smallest and most remote locations throughout the United States. On the North Fork, as in many other areas, most of the current B&Bs are housed in period buildings that reflect a bygone era. Following are images of just a few of many that now dot the North Fork.

Opposite, top: Freddy's House, Cutchogue, 2009. Freddy's House Bed-and-Breakfast is a traditional Long Island farmstead located along New Suffolk Road in the village of Cutchogue. Built in 1798 by David Tuthill, the house and grounds have operated as a farming complex ever since. In 1880, the house was enlarged with the addition of a second home that was moved from Southold and adjoined to the original Cape Cod structure. Opening their home as a B&B in 1997, Prudence and Dan Heston have worked to carefully restore the house and grounds to its respective 1798 and 1830 roots. Walking through the house, guests can step from 1798 architecture into 1880 farm life and then out the door onto a current Long Island fruit farm. *Courtesy of Freddy's House Bed-and-Breakfast.*

Opposite, bottom: The Blue Iris Bed-and-Breakfast, Cutchogue, 2009. The Blue Iris Bed-and-Breakfast was built in 2002 to appear as if it had been on the North Fork for one hundred years. The classic farmhouse design, with wraparound porch, was meticulously designed by owners Lorry and Jerry Siani with modern amenities for each of the three guestrooms, including private bathrooms, gas fireplaces and a classic parlor and dining room for guests. *Courtesy of Blue Iris Bed-and-Breakfast.*

Vintage Bed-and-Breakfast, Cutchogue, 2009. Vintage Bed-and-Breakfast is located on Skunk Lane, nearby both Bedell Cellars and Pindar Vineyards in Cutchogue. Offering three guest suites plus spa services, it is located in easy walking distance of several award-winning wineries, farm stands, shopping and the beautiful, expansive Peconic Bay Beach at the end of the street. Built in 2000 and set on more than two and a half acres, Vintage is among the newest B&Bs on the North Fork and is currently operated by Jeanne and Lou Genovese. *Courtesy of Vintage Bed-and-Breakfast.*

Andrew's Legacy Bed-and-Breakfast, Peconic, 2009. Andrew's Legacy Bed-and-Breakfast is a fourth-generation family home situated in the heart of Long Island's East End wine country. Located two houses west of Bedell Cellars, the bed-and-breakfast features antiques and family heirlooms in a sophisticated yet comfortable country setting. Guests are treated to a formal Victorian breakfast consisting of homemade jams, jellies and marmalades, fresh eggs from the backyard chickens, homemade bread and other country specialties, served from nineteenth-century silver plates in golden oak surroundings. The owners of Andrew's Legacy are descendants of the owner of the old MacNish Hotel in New Suffolk. *Courtesy of Andrew's Legacy Bed-and-Breakfast.*

Harbor Knoll, Greenport, 2009. This waterfront Dutch Colonial home with its own private beach and dock was built in 1870 as a summer home for a wealthy southern family. In the early 1950s, it was bought by Charles W. Elmer, who married a niece of General Custer's and contributed to the establishment of Custer Institute in Southold. It was bought by the Miller family in 1973 as a summer home, and following Mrs. Miller's retirement, converted to a bed-and-breakfast in 2001. With fantastic waterfront views, a wonderful garden and exquisitely decorated in the English country house style, this five-bedroom inn with separate cottage provides the perfect getaway to the North Fork. *Courtesy of Harbor Knoll Bed-and-Breakfast.*

Shorecrest, Greenport, 2007. Shorecrest Bed-and-Breakfast, a Four Square Victorian mansion, sits proudly on a beautifully landscaped acre atop a crest of land overlooking the Long Island Sound to the north and Arshamomaque Pond to the south. The house has been immaculately maintained in all its original Victorian elegance, complete with molded ten-foot ceilings and floor-to-ceiling windows and furnished with period antiques in every room. Built originally as a summer home for a wealthy New Jersey doctor, Shorecrest retains the original beach rights with private beaches and moorings to both the Long Island Sound and the bay, the former perfect for swimming, snorkeling and walking and the latter for fishing, sailing and water sports. *Courtesy of Susan and John Barnes.*

Bartlett House, Greenport, 2009. Bartlett House was built in 1908 by John J. Bartlett (1863–1922), New York assemblyman and delegate to the 1904 Republican National Convention, as a summer home for entertaining many of that period's luminaries. This large classic Revival house was built with Corinthian columns, stained-glass windows, hand-cast plaster ceilings with elegant moldings and a musician's balcony. The home remained as a family residence for nearly half a century. Then it was sold to St. Agnes Church, which operated the building for about twenty years as a convent for the nuns of the Sisters of Charity, who taught at the nearby St. Agnes School. When the nuns departed, Bartlett House suffered from abandonment and neglect. About 1982, the building was purchased by John and Linda Sabatino, who repaired and improved the structure and opened it to the public as the Bartlett House Inn Bed-and-Breakfast. The present owners, Diane and Jack Gilmore, purchased the B&B in July 2003 and continue the long established tradition of North Fork hospitality. *Courtesy of Bartlett House Bed-and-Breakfast.*

Opposite, top: Quintessentials, East Marion, 2009. Quintessentials Bed-and-Breakfast and Spa, located in East Marion, is the former Leek House, an Italianate Victorian built circa 1840, with a crowning widow's walk, by Captain Leek, who was a commercial seaman and local business entrepreneur. The house, set in an acre of beautiful gardens enhanced by a Victorian gazebo and much-photographed two-story barn, has a finely carved oak staircase, stained-glass windows, ribbon-bordered parquet floors, oak-inlaid dining room ceiling, beautifully carved oak and mahogany fireplaces and a commanding mahogany carved archway between the parlor and the library. Leek, his family and their succeeding generations lived in this fine example of a sea captain's home until its purchase by the present owner, Sylvia Daley, in 1994. *Courtesy of Quintessentials Bed-and-Breakfast.*

Opposite, bottom: Arbor View House, East Marion, 2009. Arbor View House Bed-and-Breakfast and Spa opened its doors in August 1999. It offers spa services in addition to the traditional bed-and-breakfast fare. The house, constructed about 1780, was originally a Federal-style residence and was completely renovated and doubled in size in 1863 to the current Victorian style by Captain Vail, a local whaling captain. Vail is buried in the nearby East Marion cemetery. The house is listed on the SPLIA (Society for the Preservation of Long Island Antiquities) list of historic buildings. The building has been thoroughly restored and repainted in historic hues. *Courtesy of Arbor View House Bed-and-Breakfast.*

Orient Inn, Orient, 2009. The Orient Inn was formerly the Edwards House, constructed in 1906 by Edward Edwards on land deeded to him and his brothers, George and Nathaniel. The land was transferred to them by Helen and Maria Terry, then owners of Eastholme, the large Italianate residence located across the road, which is now referred to as the Nathaniel Edwards House. It is a large, two-and-a-half-story, Shingle-style house with a gabled gambrel roof and typical Queen Anne sashes. The interior woodwork has been impeccably maintained. *Courtesy of Orient Inn Bed-and-Breakfast.*

Bibliography

Albertson, Ralph. *Romance of Jamesport.* Riverhead, NY: Riverhead News, 1944.

"American Jewish Year Book, 1913–1914." www.ajcarchives.org/AJC_DATA/Files/1913_1914_5_YearReview.pdf.

Bailey, Paul. *Long Island: A History of Two Great Counties Nassau and Suffolk in Three Volumes, Volume 1.* New York: Lewis Historical Publishing Company, 1949.

"Bed & Breakfast." en.wikipedia.org/wiki/Bed_and_breakfast.

Beers, F.W. *Atlas of Long Island.* New York: Beers, Comstock and Cline, 1873.

Belcher-Hyde, E. *Atlas of a Part of Suffolk County Long Island, New York, North side Ocean Shore.* New York: E. Belcher Hyde, 1909.

Booth, Antonia, et al. *Images of America Greenport.* Portsmouth, NH: Arcadia Publishing, 2004.

Booth, Curtis H. *Progress in Reverse.* 1970. www.frostsonli.com/Greenport%20Final%2001%20A.html.

Braden, Donna R. *Leisure and Entertainment in America.* Dearborn, MI: Henry Ford Museum & Greenfield Village, 1988.

Comes, Clarence R. "Mac Nish's Hotel, New Suffolk." *Long Island Forum* 20, no. 8 (August 1956): 142, 148.

Corwin, Elise Knapp. *Greenport: Yesterday and Today.* Mattituck, NY: Amereon House, 1972.

County Review. "Southold Hotel, Reconstructed Many Times During Past 100 Years, Torn Down to Make Way for Bank; Was Once Center of Business and Social Activities." June 17, 1926.

Craven, Charles E. *A History of Mattituck, Long Island, New York.* Mattituck, NY: Amereon Ltd., 1906, reprinted 1988.

Doughty, David. *History of Jamesport and South Jamesport.* Unpublished, copy held in the Suffolk County Historical Society, Riverhead, NY.

Ellis, David M., et al. *A History of New York State.* Cornell, NY: Cornell University Press, 1967.

Ferguson, Henry L. *Fishers Island, NY 1614–1925.* New York: Privately printed, 1925.

Fleming, Geoffrey K. *Southold.* Charleston, SC: Arcadia Publishing, 2004.

Gabriel, Ralph H. *The Evolution of Long Island.* Port Washington, NY: Ira J. Friedman Inc., 1921, reprinted 1968.

Gildersleeve, Charles. *Scrapbook.* Unpublished, copy held in the Mattituck Historical Society, Mattituck, NY.

Griffin, Augustus. *Journal.* Orient, NY: Oysterponds Historical Society, 1983.

Hall, Warren. *Pagans, Puritans, Patriots of Yesterday's Southold.* Cutchogue, NY: Cutchogue New Suffolk Historical Council, 1975.

Hart, George E. "Summer Hotels I Recall." *Long Island Forum* 13, no. 9 (September 1950): 177, 180.

Hastings, Kirk. *Doo Wop Motels.* Mechanicsburg, PA: Stakepole Books, 2007.

Heany, James, comp. *Greenporters and Where they Live in the 1930's.* 1998. Unpublished, copy held in the collection of the Oysterponds Historical Society, Orient, NY.

Horton, Lizzie. *Scrapbook.* Unpublished, copy held in the collection of the Cutchogue New Suffolk Public Library, Cutchogue, NY.

"Horton's Point House." Brochure, late nineteenth century, copy held by the Southold Free Library, Southold, NY.

Jakle, John A., et al. *The Motel in America.* Baltimore, MD: Johns Hopkins University Press, 1996.

Jefferson, Wayland. *Cutchogue, Southold's First Colony.* Cutchogue, NY: Cutchogue New Suffolk Historical Council, 1975.

Larkin, Jack. *The Reshaping of Everyday Life 1790–1840.* New York: Harper Collins, 1989.

Lawton Company. *The Southold Shelter Island Register.* Auburn, ME: Lawton Company, 1911.

Lewis Publishing Company. *Biographical and Genealogical History of Morris County New Jersey.* Vol. II. New York and Chicago: Lewis Publishing Company, 1899.

Long Island Traveler. "Jamesport." April 12, 1895, 2.

———. "Southold." July 1, 1875, 2.

"Marble Cemetery, NYC." www.nycmc.org/intermentvaults.html.

Mattituck Historical Society. *The Charles Gildersleeve Collection*. Unpublished, copy held in the collection of the Mattituck Historical Society, Mattituck, NY.

Mayne, Katherine Newell. *The History of Nassau Point*. Southold, NY: Privately printed, 1998.

"Munnatawket Hotel Brochure." www.archive.org/details/munnatawkethotel00fish.

Naylor, Natalie, ed. *Journeys on Old Long Island, Travelers' Accounts, Contemporary Descriptions, and Residents' Reminiscences 1744–1893*. Interlaken, NY: Heart of the Lakes Publishing, 2002.

New York Times. "Almarin T. Hale Dead." April 10, 1927, E8.

———. "Auction Sales." September 14, 1939, 37.

———. "Best of Breed Won by Ferguson Entry." October 19, 1928, 19.

———. "Connecticut Hotel Under New Control." April 3, 1933, 31.

———. "Fishers Island." September 3, 1911, X5.

———. "Fishers Island." June 23, 1912, X4.

———. "Fishers Island Display Ads." 1891–1917.

———. Letter to the Editor. June 25, 1893, 12.

———. Obituary Notes. January 2, 1910, 13.

"Old Coney Island Hotels." www.geocities.com/buddychai2/Brooklyn/Hotels.html.

Oysterponds Historical Society. *Landon Ledger*. Unpublished, copy held in the collection of the Oysterponds Historical Society, Orient, NY.

———. *Orient Houses*. Orient, NY: Oysterponds Historical Society, Orient, NY, 1975, reissued in 1995.

———. *Oysterponds Historical Society Research Files*, "*Hotels*." Orient, NY.

Panchyk, Richard. *Forgotten Tales of Long Island*. Charleston, SC: The History Press, 2008.

Passenger Department of LIRR. *List of Hotels and Boarding Cottages on Long Island*. New York: Long Island Railroad, 1887.

———. *Long Island Summer Homes*. New York: Long Island Railroad, 1901.

Passenger Traffic Department of LIRR. *Long Island America's Sunrise Land.* New York: Long Island Railroad, 1929.

Rackett, Dwight. *Scrapbook*. Unpublished, original held in the collection of the Oysterponds Historical Society, Orient, NY.

Ross, John. *The Food and Wine of the North Fork*. Huntington, NY: Maple Hill Press, 2005.

Sherrill, E.L., III, Jeffrey Kasner and Jeanette Rattray. *Bunker Fishery*. East Hampton, NY: Springs Historical Society, 2007.

Southold Free Library. *Hotels, Clipping Files*. Copy held in the collection of the Southold Free Library, Southold, NY.

Southold Historical Society. *Southold Historical Society Pamphlet Files*. Southold, NY.

"Southold Hotel Described by First Proprietor's Son." Copy held by the Southold Free Library, Southold, NY.

———. *Southold Historical Society Research Files "Old Village Inns."* Southold, NY.

SPLIA. *Historic Structure Inventory Form, 1987*. Copy held in the collection of the Southold Free Library, Southold, NY.

Staff and Volunteers of Sagamore Hill NHS. *Sagamore Hill*. Lawrenceburg, IN: R.L. Ruehrwein, 2000.

Stark, Thomas. *Riverhead: The Halcyon Years*. Huntington, NY: Maple Hill Press, 2005.

Suffolk Historic Newspapers. *Long Island Traveler*. shn.suffolk.lib.ny.us.

Swaney, Lois. "Prohibition—1920–1933. A Review of Enriching Local Activities During the 'Noble Experiment.'" Circa 1990 (photocopy).

Terry, Becky. "The Southold Hotel." *Peconic Bay Shopper*. August 6, 1985.

———. "Yesterday's Hotels and Boarding Houses." *Peconic Bay Shopper*. April 7, 1993, 3–10.

Tolles, Bryant F. *Summer by the Seaside: The Architecture of New England Coastal Resort Hotels, 1820–1950*. Lebanon, NH: University Press of New England, 2008.

Tooker, John. "Famous Summer Hotels." *Long Island Forum* 13, no. 7 (July 1950): 126, 130.

Tyler, Lyon Gardiner. *England in American: 1580–1652*. E-Book, released 2005. Available from www.gutenberg.org/etext/16294.

Village of Greenport Business Improvement District. *Village of Greenport Architectural Walking Tour*. Greenport, NY: North Fork Press, n.d.

Webster's New World Dictionary of the American Language. New York: World Publishing Company, 1957.

"What is a Bed & Breakfast?" bandb.about.com/cs/aspiring/a/what_is_bandb.html.

You Might Also Enjoy

101 Glimpses of the North Fork and Islands
by Rosemary McKinley
978-1-59629-657-2 • 128 pp. • Over 100 images • 5 x 7 • $14.99

The North Fork's natural riches have been seducing people for more than four hundred years. The Algonquin Indians—and, later, Dutch and English colonists—first recognized the area for its waters rich with clams and fish, its fertile soil for growing crops and its abundant forests to support shipbuilding. Hearing the ocean's call, many have long admired the inlets, creeks and bays and contrast the ruggedness of the Long Island Sound with the tranquility of Peconic Bay. In this pictorial history, local author Rosemary McKinley showcases the nautical history, idyllic seaside settings and lush landscapes of this picturesque country.

Also Available from The History Press

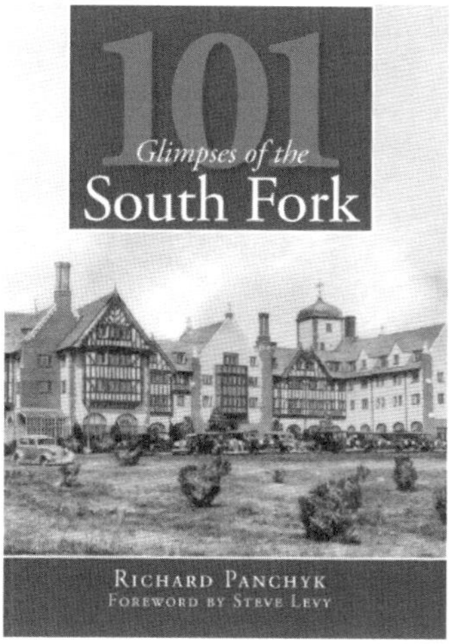

101 Glimpses of the South Fork
by Richard Panchyk

978-1-59629-670-1
128 pp. • Over 100 images • 5 x 7 • $14.99

In this pictorial history, Richard Panchyk surveys how dramatically the landscape of the South Fork has changed, from the famous Montauk Lighthouse and iconic windmills to sprawling mansions and opulent hotels, and highlights the celebrities and politicians who have graced its shores.

Southold Reminiscences:
Rural America at the Turn of the Century
by Joseph Nelson Hallock
Edited by Geoffrey K. Fleming

978-1-59629-546-9
128 pp. • over 40 images • 6 x 9 • $19.99

Southold newspaperman Joseph Hallock writes of the difficulties and pleasures of North Fork life one hundred years ago in his *Southold Reminiscences*.